# CIVIL WAR
# TRIVIA

# CIVIL WAR TRIVIA

Norman Bolotin

with Nicholle Carrière

BLUE
BIKE
BOOKS

© 2011 by Blue Bike Books
First printed in 2011 10 9 8 7 6 5 4 3 2 1
Printed in Canada

The Publisher: Blue Bike Books
Website: www.bluebikebooks.com

Library and Archives Canada Cataloguing in Publication

Bolotin, Norman, 1951–
    Civil War trivia / Norman Bolotin, Nicholle Carrière.

ISBN 978-1-926700-31-1

    1. United States—History—Civil War, 1861–1865—Miscellanea.
I. Carrière, Nicholle, 1961– II. Title.

E468.B72 2011                973.7                C2010-907633-8

*Project Director:* Nicholle Carrière
*Project Editor:* Nicholle Carrière
*Cover Image:* © Photos.com
*Photographs:* Photographs and illustrations courtesy of the Library of Congress (pp. 20, 22, 45, 49, 58, 67, 73, 85, 87, 92, 94, 101, 102, 105, 107, 110, 113, 114, 115, 116, 117, 119, 122, 123, 125, 126, 129, 131, 132, 140, 154, 162, 166, 168, 173, 185, 189, 191, 203). All other images are courtesy of the author's personal archives, some of which were used in *The Young Readers' History of the Civil War*, developed by Norman Bolotin and Christine Laing, published by Penguin/Dutton and Scholastic Books.

We acknowledge the support of the Alberta Foundation for the Arts for our publishing program.

We acknowledge the financial support of the Government of Canada through the Canada Book Fund (CBF) for our publishing activities.

Canadian    Patrimoine
Heritage    canadien

*PC:* 1

# DEDICATION

*To Bill Moylan, who never knew he sparked my interest
and helped turn a lazy junior high school student
into a Civil War historian and author*

# CONTENTS

# ACKNOWLEDGMENTS

There are many people behind the scenes who contribute to the success of a book in many ways and at many different times.

If longtime friend and publishing colleague Glenn Rollans (and my co-director for many years at the University of Chicago's Business of Publishing program) had not introduced me to Blue Bike Books, I never would have had anyone to thank for help on a project that never would have existed.

Nicholle Carrière, publisher of Blue Bike Books, was a pleasure to work with in developing this book. She demonstrated unique communications skills and patience, and precise editing acumen and conscientiousness in all aspects of the project.

Tom McCarthy, whom I first worked with to launch a new healthcare book publishing company nearly 20 years ago, is one of the most knowledgeable individuals anywhere about Civil War facts and factual nuances. The quality and depth of his personal Civil War library outstrips many institutional collections. He was, yet again, gracious in providing me complete access to his material, including unique diaries and seldom-seen, first-person accounts of both Union and Confederate soldiers. Many of the anecdotes published here have never been published before or, if so, only in obscure volumes immediately after the war.

I have written my thanks in many books before, but never have I stepped out of the professional and formal approach to doing so. Having read hundreds of acknowledgments that thank parents, spouses, siblings, college roommates, neighbors, fourth cousins, et al., I see no reason, finally, in my old age not to be myself and to thank the most important people in any book I write. I'm blessed with three terrific kids, and each one of them has had to endure questions and comments from me, and in this most recent book, each demonstrated their own writing and/or creative skills when I asked them to be sounding boards and share their thoughts. Thank you, Jacob, Zack and Hannah.

And since 1973, when we were both employed at the magazine publishing house where we met, Christine Laing has had to pit her indefatigable editorial prowess against my, shall we say, unrefined (yet creative!) use of the English language. She has repaired and rebuilt more of my manuscripts than I care to acknowledge. She managed to skirt involvement in this project because of the simultaneous deadline on the history of the World's Columbian Midway that we're coauthoring, but fielded my constant questions from across the office. She has amazing editing skill and tenacity, and living through our myriad writer-editor battles has made our years of marriage and parenting seem easy by comparison.

Over the years, our writing and development of seven other Civil War books never would have happened—and thus *Civil War Trivia* would not have existed—unless then–Dutton Children's Publisher Christopher Franceschelli had not shared my vision for providing students with illustrated history books—a startling concept in the 1980s!

The trail behind a successful book is always crowded with innovative and talented people who were helpful with this book before it even existed. I'm sorry I do not have space to acknowledge the many colleagues whose efforts previously laid an important foundation for this title. No book happens in a vacuum, either in the present or the past. Thanks to those many book people who were integral in making *Civil War Trivia* a fine book.

# INTRODUCTION

The Civil War, in many ways, was deeply rooted in the very beginnings of the United States, in the Declaration of Independence and the Constitution. Those documents are some of the most brilliant writing ever undertaken, and regardless of how some people today or during the Civil War may have chosen to criticize Thomas Jefferson because he was a slaveholder, his writing not only helped form a nation, but provided the foundation for other countries and countless men and women seeking to delineate human rights.

In the Declaration of Independence, Jefferson wrote:

> *We hold these truths to be self-evident, that all men are created equal, that they are endowed by their Creator with certain unalienable Rights, that among these are Life, Liberty and the pursuit of Happiness. That to secure these rights, Governments are instituted among Men, deriving their just powers from the consent of the governed, That whenever any Form of Government becomes destructive of these ends, it is the Right of the People to alter or to abolish it…*

In the antebellum South, leaders believed that states had the right to make decisions about their individual state governments and to continue slavery as it existed when the United States was formed. Despite the near perfection of the founding documents, they, like any written record, simple or profound, are products of their times and of the perspectives of the writers within the context of the period of history in which they were written.

In the heated senatorial debates between Stephen A. Douglas and Abraham Lincoln in 1858, both men clung to the rights given citizens by the Constitution. Douglas pointed out that the founding fathers did not consider slaves as men, but as property, a viewpoint no one could argue. That is what the new country believed in 1776 and what the slave states still believed in 1858, where the country allowed slavery to exist. Where there was no slavery, free black men still lacked the rights of citizenship. Lincoln eloquently maintained that even if not given the rights of a citizen, the black man in America still had "the right to eat the bread, without the leave of anybody else, which his own hand earns [and in doing so] he is my equal and the equal of Judge Douglas, and the equal of every living man."

When the founding fathers crafted those roadmaps for building a new government of the people, by the people and for the people, they addressed citizens of the new country who were men, not women and not men of color. They were breaking away from British rule, and in doing so, they were establishing new laws and declaring new rights and demanding an improved quality of life. No doubt, 80 years later, Jefferson would have agreed with Lincoln on slavery and states' rights. Well before the 1860s and the Civil War, Americans and many around the globe had advanced their views on human rights, and slavery was being abolished or questioned throughout the world. It was time in the United States, as well.

Lincoln and Douglas, like so many since, have argued the meaning of the Constitution and the rights bestowed upon men. The founding fathers understood that change would occur, and that is why there is a mechanism for amending the Constitution. The 13th Amendment did just that during the Civil War by abolishing slavery in the United States.

The disagreements between the North and the South had been brewing for decades. There were vast differences in their ways of life, their views on trade and their politics.

But nothing stirred more conflict and inspired more passion than the issue of states' rights—most importantly, the right of a state to declare itself "slave" or "free." Lincoln did not want to be viewed solely in the role of abolitionist, but he was a strong constitutional attorney, and it became impossible to separate constitutional issues from slavery.

By the time the 1860 election occurred, Lincoln had become a major voice for the abolishment of slavery, even if it was not his original intent. He desperately sought to preserve the Union and to avoid war.

Lincoln's famous "House Divided" speech in his debates with Douglas in 1858 clearly stated that a country split apart could not survive, which meant, of course, that the South could not maintain slavery and remain part of the country. And vocal Southerners reiterated his very statements and said that if Lincoln was elected, war was inevitable. Of course, had any other candidate carried the banner for the new Republican Party, the South's comments would have been the same.

Once Lincoln was elected, some states left the Union and formed the Confederate States of America, which they declared to be a free and independent country. In his inaugural address, Lincoln said he had no intention of invading southern states or of forcing those that allowed slavery to abolish it, but he wanted to stop the spread of slavery and, above all, preserve the union. Attempts for peaceful compromise failed and, on April 12, 1861, Confederate forces opened fire on Fort Sumter, signaling the beginning of what was to be four years of a war far bloodier and more destructive than either side could have imagined.

From its army to the general public, the North believed its vast numbers and military superiority would quickly still the Confederate rebels. The war would, no doubt, be short. But soon there were millions of soldiers engaged in battle, and the Union was not handily defeating the South as expected; to the contrary, early battles actually favored the Confederates—and the South believed it could win the war.

When the war was over, the United States had lost an innocence that could never be regained. Virtually every family from Maine to Florida, Texas to Illinois, lost husbands and brothers, fathers and sons, cousins and uncles. Entire cities and huge pieces of the landscape, homes, plantations and farms—the majority in the South—all vanished.

But somehow, the South and the North rebuilt and moved forward. The war was overseen by one of our finest presidents: Abraham Lincoln. Reconstruction was overseen by one of our worst: Andrew Johnson. But the country survived.

What would Jefferson have thought about the issues of slavery and the Civil War? What would Lincoln, Washington and so many others think of our progress today?

For all the ethereal discussions, for the massive impact the Civil War had on the nation, our goal in *Civil War Trivia* is not to emulate what has been told in hundreds of comprehensive books on the war. Nor did we have any desire to provide a one-dimensional compendium of staggering facts, figures and statistics.

Our goal is to take a refreshingly different approach, even light-hearted at times, in presenting the stories and interesting details that paint the pictures of the Civil War at the frontlines and behind the scenes. Some may be facts you've heard many times but are framed here in a different light. Others, we hope, will surprise or astonish you. And, yes, some may turn your stomach. But at the heart of the trivia is the story of millions of Americans, divided by politics, fighting to protect what they so passionately believed in.

# Important Pieces in Assembling This Civil War Puzzle

Trivia means something different to everyone. Some may think of it as a compilation of simple quizzes, questions and tidbits. We think of it as a world of great stories and unique tales, boiled down into an easily read format. *Civil War Trivia* is not just the trivia you answer on the back of a game card, but by definition something much more compelling. The origin of the word "trivia" is the Latin term *trivium*, meaning "a place where three roads meet." And we have taken that definition to guide us, so that rather than simple facts and a journey down one road, we have selected many complex tales that occurred down the many varied roads of the Civil War and the most tumultuous time in American history.

We went in many different directions to provide important numbers (but not just lists of numbers and nothing else) and statistical tables but did our best to find statistics and lists that are unusual and that have a story to share, as well. We combed the Internet and libraries for unusual stories and anecdotes. And we went beyond that, to a marvelous private library devoted to Civil War books, periodicals, private letters and diaries, dating from the war up through modern analyses and opinions. But the bulk of the library consists of books from the war years through the years immediately after. The curator of that private collection, Thomas McCarthy, was kind enough to allow us unlimited access in publishing this book.

Other material came from the author's own archives of Civil War newspapers, documents, letters, and other ephemera.

The photos used here, from a variety of sources, including the author's archives and the Library of Congress, were selected to provide you with an important supplement to the text, so that you could enjoy both the words and important pictures taken by the many professional photographers who followed the men and women taking part in the Civil War, from the battlefield to the relative safety of cities nearby. Photography was a relatively new art and technology at that time, and these photographers provided us a brilliant means of studying the war.

# A Few Questions of Civil War Civility

A few names and references might cause confusion in this look at the seldom-trivial trivia of the Civil War. There are no intentional tongue twisters, but, unintentionally, one never knows. Here are a few items to note, since you might not see the definition or explanation before the first use of the term.

Many references simply aren't what one might expect. The word "contraband" is clearly defined in the text, but it had its own definition and use in the Civil War, and it's nothing from a spy thriller or World War II report on smuggling. In fact, "contraband" refers to escaped slaves and provided a way for Northern soldiers to label runaway slaves to prevent having to return them to their "owners."

During the Civil War, there were too many disgusting, disparaging references used in identifying slaves and/or African Americans. Certainly, the term "Negro" was not intended in any way to be derogatory. Our usage in this book is simply to refer to the African American slaves and free men and women as "black" people. Less cumbersome than African American, the term is accepted today and was also used during the Civil War.

The most famous sea battle in American history was the world's first battle between iron ships, the Union's *Monitor* and the Confederate *Merrimac*. But the usage is not entirely correct, either, though accepted. The original hull of the ship on which the Confederate States Ship (CSS) ironclad was built was a wooden Union ship, the *Merrimack*, spelled with a *k*. The CSS christened the new ironclad as the *Virginia* and, to be historically correct, the battle was between the *Monitor* and the *Virginia*. To make things even more confusing, subsequent vessels similar in design to the *Monitor* became known as "monitors."

# Major Civil War Battles

Free States

Border States

Confederate States

Major Battles

Major Cities

In the western and central U.S. (not shown), Texas was a Confederate state, whereas Oregon, California and Kansas were Union. During the war, West Virginia and Nevada became states and joined the Union. The four slave states—Delaware, Maryland, Kentucky and Missouri—that remained with the Union were known as "Border States" and their neutrality was vital to the Northern war effort. Oklahoma, then the Indian Territory and not a state, is included in some maps because its Native population was strongly Confederate.

# WHEN COMPROMISES SUCCEED...OR DON'T

*Slavery has always been put forth as the cause of the American Civil War, but, in fact, the issue could have been turnips, taxes or transportation. The cause of the war was states' rights. States in the South believed they had the right to determine their own course of action, not unlike political battles 150 years later. Could a state allow slavery within its borders? Or could the federal government tell South Carolina or any other state how it should govern itself? Southerners said that the election of Abraham Lincoln as president would mean war—and it did.*

## The Missouri Compromise of 1820

Even with a constitution, nothing is permanent; no matter how strong the federal law or the Constitution, there's always a way to change it, and change just isn't necessarily good.

The Missouri Compromise of 1820 prohibited any new states entering the Union after the Louisiana Purchase, with the exception of Missouri, from having slavery—and so it was for three decades.

### The Kansas-Nebraska Act of 1854 Made Civil War Inevitable

The Kansas-Nebraska Act effectively repealed the Missouri Compromise. The bill was intended to boost settlement in the West and spur the growth of the country. Two new territories, Kansas and Nebraska, were formed, but Illinois senator Stephen A. Douglas, the author of the bill, included a clause calling for "popular sovereignty," allowing the residents of a state to choose whether or not slavery would be permitted. Douglas hoped the bill would improve relations between the North and the South, but the bill had the opposite effect.

## Camp and Outpost Duty for Infantry

The excerpts included throughout this book are from a small manual titled *Camp and Outpost Duty for Infantry with standing orders, extracts from the revised regulations for the army, rules for health, maxims for soldiers and duties of officers as assembled by Major General Daniel Butterfield.* It was owned during the war by Lieutenant Edward M. Rand, of the 27th Maine Volunteers, who dated this book when he acquired it in Chantilly, Virginia, on May 12, 1863. This was the height of the bloodiest period in the Civil War, leading up to the Battle of Gettysburg less than two months down the road. Rand later donated the book to the Military Order of the Loyal Legion of the United States Library in Maine in 1903.

## New Republican Party Formed Out of Opposition to the Kansas-Nebraska Act

A new political party arose out of the aftermath of the Kansas-Nebraska Act's passage. One Illinois attorney, Abraham Lincoln, left his Whig affiliation and moved to the new party. He battled Douglas in two elections, for a U.S. Senate Seat from Illinois in 1858 and for the presidency in 1860.

## One Nation Not Very Far Removed

One major peculiarity of this war, in which two "countries" fought terrible battles for four years, is that the countries had been one just prior to the outbreak of the war. While many civil wars occur between political factions in the same country, the American Civil War was fought between the United States and the separate and instantly formed Confederate States. In terms of a civil war, it was unusual, and the proximity of the countries and their governments was dramatic.

U.S. Signal Corps headquarters in Vicksburg, Mississippi

∽

Washington, DC, effectively "in" Virginia if not part of it, was one capital, whereas Richmond, so near to the South, became the capital city of the newly established Confederacy.

The Whig Party was short-lived in the U.S. It was formed in 1834 as opposition to Andrew Jackson's policies of a strong presidential office that many considered too strong. The name "Whig" was chosen to remind Americans of the Loyalist Whigs during the Revolutionary War, which in turn had come from the British anti-tyranny Whig Party. In its short life, the Whig Party saw two presidents elected, James Polk and Zachary Taylor. Key Whig leaders were Henry Clay and Daniel Webster, and Lincoln found this party the closest to his own strong constitutional views. The party disappeared when members could not decide between the anti-slavery position of the North and the states' rights/pro-slavery position of the South. Lincoln switched to the new Republican Party, which was clearly anti-slavery. It was the Republicans' first foray into a presidential election in 1860, which, of course, Lincoln won.

Even the first battle, at Fort Sumter, resulted in a Union fort in a Southern location being captured by the country of which it was physically a part.

Both the Union and the Confederacy guarded their seats of government, and battles raged all around. For most of the war, neither side attacked the other's capital until the North captured Richmond in April 1865.

When the Confederates threatened Washington and invaded Northern territory, it was in the central part of Pennsylvania—the thrust into the North turned back with the North's victory at Gettysburg. Ironically, the move was strategically intended to "invade" the North and move toward the capital. In actuality, spies and undercover Confederates were on occasion behind enemy lines and in the city of Washington. And, on other occasions, battles raged ridiculously close to the capital.

## Camp and Outpost Duty for Infantry

Neither the picket-guards nor the outposts will ever be allowed to occupy a house, unless so directed by the field officer of the day.

# THE UNITED STATES BY THE NUMBERS

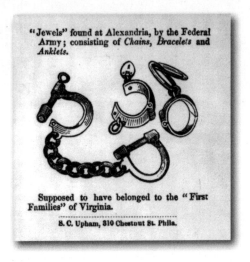

The "jewels" of the First Families of Virginia, consisting of slave chains and shackles; from an illustrated Union envelope

## The Slave Population

When the Civil War broke out, the population of the United States—North and South—was not quite 31.5 million, and of the greatest concern to the Southern states was the slave population, about four million people (though they were considered property, not human beings, in the South). That four million was about 12.5 percent of the *total* population—combined North and South—of the United States.

## Population Loss

The Civil War ravaged the country in myriad ways, but often picturing the numbers helps us comprehend the enormity of the event.

A total of two percent of the country's population, North and the South, would lie dead before a truce was reached.

An estimated 600,000 men were lost in battle, to disease and in accidents on the battlefields, behind the scenes and in prisoner-of-war camps in both the North and South.

## A Young Man's Endeavor

According to the records of the U.S. Army, at least 25 "men" out of the 2.3 million serving the Union were younger than 10 years old. Another 300 were not yet teenagers. Some 100,000 of those enlisted were 15 years of age, and about the same number were 16. A whopping 70 percent of the enlisted total of the Union forces (or 1.6 million soldiers) were under the age of 23.

Young men posing in Union hats and belts but no other official uniform.
It was common for young recruits to pose for pictures
before joining their units and going to war.

Somewhere deep in the cavernous records of the War Department, there is probably a delineation of the average age of the casualties, both dead and wounded. Quite likely, the numbers who died of disease or in prisoner-of-war camps (primarily of disease and starvation) were older enlistees who were statistically more likely to have been physically weaker, but there are no official numbers to substantiate this.

Government and private records estimate that some 300 women disguised as males fought alongside men during the Civil War. The last veterans of the war lived nearly a century after it ended—the last Union soldier passed away in 1956; the last Confederate soldier died three years later.

## Camp and Outpost Duty for Infantry

Great care should always be exercised to conceal, if possible, the position of the men, and the fact that they are watching, noting or sketching any thing with regard to the position of the enemy or country.

## Similar Losses on Both Sides

The Union prisoner-of-war camps were miserable, but the Southern camps were inhumane and far worse. Still, the numbers were not much different.

In the North, an estimated 215,000 Southern troops were incarcerated during the war, while the Confederates held "only" 200,000 Union men. In the North, 26,000 died while in captivity (12.1 percent); in the South, 30,000 died while imprisoned (15 percent). But the numbers cannot begin to tell the story of the horrors that the prisoners of war endured.

# Enough Manpower to Win a War

During the course of the war, an estimated 3.6 million Americans were in uniform, 2.2 million in the North and 1.4 million in the South—11.4 percent of the entire country's men, women and children, white and black.

Of the 2.2 million Union soldiers, sailors and marines, 180,000 were free black men and 3530 were Native Americans; the latter suffered approximately 1000 casualties (wounded or killed), or 28.3 percent of the total number enlisted. And those numbers paled in comparison to the number killed by U.S. troops in the Indian Wars that consumed the decade that followed the Civil War.

Recent enlistees drilling

# BEFORE LINCOLN ASSUMED THE PRESIDENCY

## Preserving the Union

Hundreds of books have been written about Abraham Lincoln and thousands about the Civil War. Try as detractors might to find flaws in his character, Lincoln was a man of his times and highly successful in one of the most difficult periods in U.S. history.

As president, he stated that his foremost goal was to preserve the Union, which he did. Secondarily, he wanted to put an end to slavery, even though he made it clear that this was not something he was prepared to do prior to assuming the presidency.

Lincoln's 272 words—barely three minutes of "appropriate remarks" at Gettysburg—have become the most-quoted and recited speech in American history. He was prepared to deal with difficult task of Reconstruction and putting the fragmented and sorely damaged country back together, but days after the war ended, he was assassinated by fanatic John Wilkes Booth.

Lincoln's life has been studied in great detail and an exhaustive biography is beyond the scope of this book, but a few of the more important facts about his political life are given below. Contemporary readers should be aware that the general policies of 19th-century Republicans might be more closely aligned with current Democrats, whereas the 1860s Democrats were more representative of the current conservative Republicans.

☞ Lincoln was one of the first framers of the new Republican Party that emerged after the long-standing Whigs crumbled.

☞ He was only the second Republican nominated for the Senate.

☞ In the 1856 national election, Lincoln was *second* in the balloting for selection of the vice presidential candidate.

☞ Nominated to run for the Senate as a Republican, Lincoln issued his famous "House Divided" speech in which he stated: "I believe this government cannot endure permanently half slave and half free. I do not expect the Union to be dissolved—I do not expect the house to fall—but I expect it will cease to be divided."

☞ Although he never claimed to be an abolitionist, he was motivated to save the Union at whatever cost.

☞ Lincoln served in the Illinois House of Representatives and in the U.S. House as well.

☛ A patent in his name is on file with the U.S. Patent Office for a device to be used to raise boats in waterways.

☛ Perhaps Lincoln's most famous political series of speeches and his foray into the national political limelight came not while running for president, but in his legendary battle with Stephen Douglas for the U.S. Senate seat from Illinois in 1858. Lincoln lost the election, but the national stage on which he and Douglas debated vaulted him into national prominence and was very likely responsible for his election as president in 1860.

☛ Douglas, a consummate politician and supporter of states' rights, backed Lincoln after the latter was elected president in 1860. Douglas died shortly thereafter, at the beginning of the Civil War.

☛ Lincoln stated his priorities clearly, declaring that his paramount objective in the struggle was to save the Union, not to either save or destroy slavery: "If I could save the Union without freeing any slave I would do it, and if I could save it by freeing all the slaves I would do it; and if I could save it by freeing some and leaving others alone I would also do that. What I do about slavery, and the colored race, I do because I believe it helps to save the Union; and what I forbear, I forbear because I do not believe it would help to save the Union."

☛ Frederick Douglass, the former slave and a major force against slavery and for the improvement of black civil rights for the rest of the century, once observed that Lincoln was "the first great man that I talked with in the United States freely who in no single instance reminded me I was a Negro."

## Camp and Outpost Duty for Infantry

If the commander is not at the head of his troops when they are to march, the next in rank puts the column in motion.

## "I Wanted to Wring the Necks of Those Little Brats..."

"They never disturbed the serenity of their father, but many a time I wanted to wring the necks of those little brats and pitch them out of the windows!" said Billy Herndon, Lincoln's partner in their law practice in Springfield, Illinois, in the 1850s in reference to his partner's children. The firm was named Lincoln and Herndon, not Herndon and Lincoln, so Lincoln's partner, and even longer-tenured friend, deferred. He liked the boys, he said, but felt their father gave them run of the office, which Lincoln never denied.

And Herndon never complained to Lincoln when Tad and Willie were busy racing through the office.

## Would Lincoln Actually Call Someone a "Liar"?

"[He] has set about seriously trying to make the impression that when we meet at different places, I am literally in his clutches— that I am a poor, helpless, decrepit mouse, and that I can do nothing at all...I don't want to quarrel with him—to call him a liar—but when I come square up to him, I don't know what else to call him."

Lincoln, who became continually more angered at the methods of Stephen Douglas during their debates, had that to say at his fifth debate with Douglas on September 18, 1858, in Charleston, Illinois. It was these debates that brought Lincoln to the forefront of American politics, even though he lost the election by a narrow margin. He then went on to win the presidency, of course, over Douglas and others two years later.

## Camp and Outpost Duty for Infantry

When a soldier without arms, or with side-arms only, meets an officer, he is to raise his hand to the right side of the visor of his cap, palm to the front, elbow raised as high as the shoulder, looking at the same time in a respectful and soldier-like manner at the officer, who will return the compliment thus offered.

## Douglas and Douglass—Two Very Different Points of View

Stephen Douglas, the "Little Giant"—short in stature but a powerful leader—was a well-known senate proponent for popular sovereignty. He was a strong orator and a relentless opponent as Lincoln discovered, but the mild-mannered Lincoln was generally acknowledged to have won the debates. After Lincoln defeated Douglas (one *s*) for the presidency, his former opponent—always on the side of democracy— supported Lincoln strongly. Sadly, less than two months later, having just turned 48 years old, Douglas died unexpectedly as the war began.

Frederick Douglass (with a double *s*) was a former slave who became one of the most influential black men in the country, working for civil rights for former slaves. He was many things in the battle for equality, especially articulate and persistent.

# A Matter of Debate

The Lincoln–Douglas debates have stood the test of time as the most powerful series of political debates in this country. There were seven debates—in seven of nine Illinois districts—since the combatants had already appeared individually in the other two. At the time, U.S. senators were elected by state legislatures rather than popular vote, so Lincoln and Douglas were stumping for the votes of each district. The debates drew national attention and papers sent stenographers to capture the speeches verbatim. And there was a lot of speaking. The debates were structured so that one man had an hour to speak, followed by the other speaking for 90 minutes, and then concluded with the first receiving an additional 30 minutes.

Lincoln's famous "House Divided" speech is the most quoted of all the debates, but the two men verbally jousted seven times, and though Lincoln never considered himself a strict abolitionist, by the time the debating was through, Lincoln was seen as the great anti-slavery candidate and Douglas the opposite, even though he was battling primarily for states' rights, not slavery, per se.

## Camp and Outpost Duty for Infantry

The outposts and sentinels will never be allowed to sleep at their posts.

# A NATION DIVIDED

## Could War Be Averted?

Washington, DC, January 6, 1861—"The excitement to-day is somewhat increased," reported the *New York Times*. On that day, the caucus of Border Free and Slave States agreed on four points:

1. A jury trial would be provided to an escaped slave…in the state from which he or she escaped. (A bonus for the slave? Not!)

2. Kansas should be admitted to the Union immediately as a state.

3. The North would remain free of slavery forever, and in the South, Congress would not interfere with slavery. (Hmmm?)

4. Once any territory of at least 60,000 square miles had a population of at least 100,000 people, its citizens could vote on whether to be a free or a slave state.

Despite all the rhetoric, no progress was made to avert war. The statement was, in fact, just a meaningless mandate from a powerless group with at least a lofty purpose, if not ideals.

### There Was More than Just North and South

Lincoln once said that he *hoped* to have God on his side but *had* to have Kentucky!

As war loomed, there was more than just North and South at issue. The so-called Border States consisted of Kentucky (crucial for control of the Ohio River), Maryland (which surrounded Washington, DC, on three sides; the fourth side was bordered by Virginia), Missouri and Delaware. Slaves were permitted in these states, but the states wanted to remain neutral and not secede. And although Lincoln wanted their support, he desperately needed at least their neutrality rather than their opposition.

John Brown's court arraignment, October 1859

# The Abolitionist Who Nearly Single-handedly Guaranteed There Would be a Civil War

John Brown, a religious zealot and anti-slavery advocate, almost single-handedly set the anti-slavery movement back a decade. Described as dishonest, a thief and crazy, Brown seemed to see himself as a combination of perhaps Moses and the Pied Piper of Hamlin. He constantly quoted scriptures and federal law—whether it was appropriate or not— and vowed publicly to free slaves and fight back against those who had murdered and mistreated them. Although most Northerners preferred peaceful resistance to pro-slavery advocates, Brown was unsatisfied with the pacifism they displayed and demanded violent action in response to aggression on the part of the South.

Brown managed to put himself and his sons squarely in the middle of conflicts in Kansas between pro- and anti-slavery supporters, and against the "bushwhackers" and Southern partisan raiders, who seemed to think that their Confederate mandate to act "under the radar" as agents for the Confederacy included robbing and murdering in Kansas.

As "Free-Staters" and pro-slavery supporters carried out more and more violence, in May 1856, Brown and his men retaliated against a killing by dragging five men from their homes and hacking them to death with swords. The violence spiraled upward after that.

In August, when pro-slavery forces killed one of Brown's sons and a neighbor near Pottawatonie, Kansas, Brown took his force of fewer than 40 men into the woods to lay in wait for the pro-slavery supporters to return, which they did with nearly 300 men. Brown's forces killed 20 and wounded 40 before scattering. Brown became a hero to many abolitionists and garnered newspaper headlines in both the North and the South. Suddenly, he was well known, based on his military prowess when outnumbered seven to one.

The Missouri troops who had attacked Brown continued on and burned the town of Pottawatonie, and their attacks on the Kansas settlements of the Free-Staters only inflamed the issue more in the eyes of Northern abolitionists, which resulted in strong financial support and weapons for Brown and his followers.

Brown received support from several powerful men in Congress and others, which was only provided as long as it was kept secret. Brown held a "Constitutional Convention" for his anti-slavery organization in Chatham, Ontario, a community of 6000, one-third of which were escaped slaves. They elected officers and wrote "A Declaration of Liberty by

## Camp and Outpost Duty for Infantry

If the movements of the enemy are reported, confusion may arise from saying "to the right" or "to the left." Say "to OUR right" or "to OUR left" and "to the enemy's right" or "to the enemy's left."

the Representatives of the Slave Population of the United States of America." Brown was commander-in-chief, and of the various officers, one was titled "Secretary of War," which is somewhat indicative of Brown's intentions to carry the abolitionist fight both figuratively and literally.

He gave no one, including his financial backers, an indication of his 1859 plans to attack Harpers Ferry, Virginia. He was sure that if he mounted a military attack, he could arm and arrange for support from thousands of slaves whom he was sure would revolt and help him. Instead of the 4500-man brigade he planned to lead in an attack on the U.S. military armory complex of several buildings at Harpers Ferry, he had a total of 21 men, including three free black men, one freed slave and one fugitive slave. The armory contained more than 100,000 weapons, with which the already well-armed Brown planned to wage war against pro-slavery factions. The weapons were intended for the large army of freed and escaped slaves that never materialized.

The fact that just one person was inside to guard the armory should have made Brown's paltry force more than adequate, but the abolitionist leader and his men were trapped inside by the townspeople, who then exchanged gunfire with Brown's forces, killing another of his sons, and held the would-be revolutionaries until federal troops arrived.

Brown was tried in Virginia under state law rather than in federal court, found guilty and subsequently hanged. However, he succeeded in a larger sense, driving a wedge between North and South and, in the minds of many, making the Civil War an inevitability.

Brown was supported silently by pro-abolitionists, but he had an incredible collection of people with whom he met who continued to defend his actions in the years that followed his death. Among them were Ralph Waldo Emerson, Walt Whitman and Frederick Douglass, who called Brown a braver advocate of freedom for slaves than himself.

In simple coincidence, federal troops sent to take over the armory and later to defend it and remove Brown were under the direction of Robert E. Lee, and Jeb Stuart and Stonewall Jackson were also both involved—and, of course, at the time, all three were U.S. Army officers.

Brown's legacy has been incredibly polarized. For a century and a half, he has been alternately revered and reviled, but even those who supported what he did often questioned whether or not his actions were rational. Regardless, his very clearly stated goals were to help bring about freedom for slaves in America, through revolt and military action, if necessary. Period.

He was hanged on December 2, 1859. The Civil War began with the attack on Fort Sumter 16 months later.

## Camp and Outpost Duty for Infantry

Always eat at regular houses; neglect in this tends to indigestion, diarrhea, etc.

# WHEN SECESSION CAME, THERE WAS NO COURSE BUT WAR

## The Vote that Started It All

A total of 169 South Carolina delegates, meeting at a specially called state convention on December 20, 1860, voted unanimously at 1:15 PM "to dissolve the Union between the State of South Carolina and other States united with her under the compact entitled 'The Constitution of the United States of America.'"

The other states that formed the Confederacy followed suit shortly thereafter.

## The Second Highest Vote to Leave the United States

South Carolina's state convention was ultimately the only vote for secession that was unanimous. The second highest vote total (by percentage) was Texas, with 166–7 (96 percent in favor of secession). Texas also held a popular vote in which its citizens were overwhelmingly in favor of secession, but certainly by nowhere near the same percentage, 46,129 to 14,697 (75.8 percent in favor).

## One Key "No" Vote in Texas

Sam Houston, governor of the state of Texas and, of course, a hero in the state's earlier fight for its own independence, did not want to join the Confederacy. He wanted Texas to revert to its independent status as a republic. His own state government rejected his ideas, removed him from the office of governor and seceded!

# PREPARING FOR WAR AT THE GRASSROOTS LEVEL

## Looking for a Fair Price for Southern Real Estate

Once South Carolina had seceded and declared itself a newly independent republic (until the secession of other states resulted in the Confederate States of America being formed, South Carolina was a republic unto itself according to its own declaration), it sent commissioners to Washington to negotiate the purchase of federal property that remained in South Carolina, specifically Forts Moultrie and Sumter. This "generous" offer apparently was made in earnest, but became moot when the new Confederate States were formed and attacked and captured the forts to start the Civil War.

## A Bounty for Service and a Way Out for Those with Money

In general, many regard the idea that those who were able to afford it could pay others to enlist in their place—essentially buying their way out of the draft—with vociferous displeasure. Well, yes, but…Typical cases were wealthy or well-to-do draftees who could pay to have someone take their place in the army, depending on circumstances. There was also a bounty system, which was much more complex. Often, a regiment being assembled would be financed by a businessman in need of a volunteer to take his place, or perhaps he would be forming a troop out of patriotism and vanity, creating a neighborhood unit to join the loyal cause, and would offer monetary compensation to anyone willing to enlist.

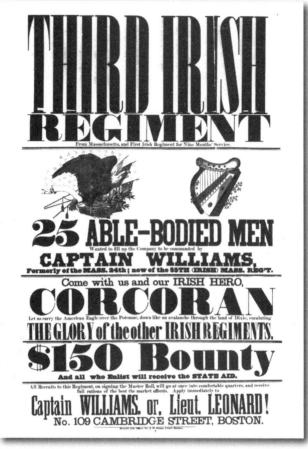

A broadside offering a bounty for enlistees to Corcoran's 3rd Irish Regiment

Regardless of the reason behind the cash, the advertisements enticing men to join a unit were quite clear about what its backer (or backers) had on the table in competitive payments in an effort to build the best unit possible.

Regiments listed their war records, their strong ethnic or cultural background and appealed to the individual pride of the enlistee, while still making the revenue a key message.

## Camp and Outpost Duty for Infantry

Sentinels will be posted from each outpost every hour. They will patrol their beats constantly after nightfall in such a manner that they will observe the sentinels on their right and left, that men in motion will guard the whole line. Nothing occurring near the lines can escape their notice and vigilance.

In New York, for example, the Brooklyn Monitors, Company A, Senatorial Regiment, advertised that it had just 20 openings remaining in a 100-man company that would be the finest and best-equipped group of volunteers being formed in Brooklyn. "A committee of gentlemen of wealth have pledged themselves to take care of the families" of the troops, and each man was remunerated with a $235 bounty—$135 of which was paid in cash at enlistment.

Thus, the soldiers were being given a bonus roughly equal to about a year and a half's salary for a soldier to enlist. What could you do with $235 at the time? Buy 100 acres of farmland, including a small cabin...or mail a letter every day for three years. And if the soldier was a city worker, he could use $235 to pay for a room with meals for eight years!

The 69th New York State Militia's advertisement stated that the "regiment that so nobly distinguished itself on the field of Bull Run...will be encamped on Staten Island, a position highly favorable to the health and good condition of the men." The bounty was $250—$150 upon enlistment and $100 at the end of the war.

Corcoran's Irish Legion, 5th Regiment, offered enlistees a $250 bounty and sought men of "good Irish character."

Whatever the underlying reason, it was a competitive advertising environment and did exactly what the government wanted—the advertisements appealed to the loyalty and patriotism of young men, encouraging them to fight for their country while offering substantial monetary compensation. It was noble gesture and also a well-funded one.

## Maryland Draftees

Once a draft was in place during the Civil War, there were more than a few who tried to avoid it. Some men enlisted to "help" the draftees and were more than willing to go to war themselves in return for collecting a substantial bounty payment. One farmer had his $1100 farm mortgage paid off and his wife was given $250 cash because he was willing to go in a draftee's place.

In the same area, a federal representative called on a farmhouse looking for the "men of the house." When the woman there responded that there were no men, the officer replied, "You cannot tell me where I can find Billy Bray?" She then directed him to the barn, and he returned saying he had found no one. After a thorough search of the farm and the nearby small town, no one admitted to knowing Billy, let alone his whereabouts. The case was closed when the man returned to the farm and was told that Billy *was* indeed on the premises—he was the family's jackass and apparently the only male on the draft roster. As you can imagine, avoiding the draft was a bit easier in the Civil War than, say, during the 20th century.

# Loyalty and Disloyalty Both Showed Their Colors

In a major scandal that rocked the government before Lincoln's election, Secretary of War (under President Buchanan) John Floyd engineered the shipment of "American" weapons to "American garrisons" in the South, including several that were not yet operational. He was finally caught when he tried to have 113 cannons shipped south from Pittsburgh.

By the time Lincoln was in office and the country was at war, the South had huge caches of weapons at forts and garrisons of the federal government within the Southern states. The Confederate army, of course, confiscated all weapons, facilities and munitions; without them, the Confederacy would have been sorely lacking when the war started. The Confederate army also had a new general—former U.S. Secretary of War Floyd.

It was but one of the scandals and military disasters that Lincoln inherited on the doorstep of war. Every incoming president complains about the status of the government with which he has been left, but Lincoln was handed a government with horrible flaws in the military, finance and numerous other areas. He certainly did not need the scandals, dishonesty and depletions of military stores when war was imminent.

## Fair Pay for Some Tough Work!

In this war, there was no easy ride for officers; they lost their lives, from lieutenants to generals, leading their men in battle. Privates were paid just $13 per month until given a raise to $16 the year before the war ended. Officers' monthly salaries were:

| | |
|---|---|
| Lieutenants | $105.50 |
| Captains | $115.50 |
| Majors | $169 |
| Colonels | $212 |
| Generals (one to three stars) | $315 to $758 |

Southern soldiers were generally paid 10 to 15 percent less, but they were promoted more rapidly. Unfortunately, one needs money to pay salaries, and the South was in a constant state of near bankruptcy, so soldiers were paid infrequently at best.

## Congressional Budget Appropriations

In 1860, with war looming, the U.S. Congress passed $55 million in budget appropriations, which included (in part) very important allocations for the military:

| | |
|---:|:---|
| Army | $15,183,070 |
| Navy | $10,461,030 |
| Legislative, judicial and executive | $6,200,963 |
| Post office | $5,007,425 |
| Diplomatic | $1,168,380 |
| Pensions | $ 849,000 |
| Military academy | $ 183,692 |

### Camp and Outpost Duty for Infantry

Care should be taken to have the camps always pitched with regularity and neatness. It adds much to the comfort of the men.

# THE NATION BEFORE SECESSION

Abraham Lincoln's inauguration in front of the under-construction Capitol Building, March 4, 1861

## Elect Lincoln and You Choose War

There was little doubt that with the election of Abraham Lincoln, some of Southern states were determined to force war upon the nation. But from the November 1860 election through April 1861, political banter was the only battle underway. Yet despite the apparent, if not obvious, inevitability of war, the North was ill prepared. When war came, the military of the United States was underfinanced and poorly manned, and with secession, garrisons, weapons and men in the South were quickly subtracted from that already weak number. Amazingly, the response was slow, until secession finally came and the war began with the attack on Fort Sumter on April 12, 1861. Even though the federal budget had included $25 million for the army and navy, it was just a dent in the total needed to go to war.

Officers of the 139th Pennsylvania Infantry

## Pennsylvania Tries to Arm Its Militia

In early April 1861, before war broke out, the governor of Pennsylvania sent an impassioned message to the state legislature: "There are numerous companies without necessary arms, and of the arms that are distributed, few are provided with modern appliances to render them serviceable.

Military organizations of a formidable character, which seem not to be demanded by an existing public exigency, have been formed in certain of the States."

Since the federal government had a standing army and navy that was too small to handle war, the first and immediate increase in troops would be a calling to arms of the states' militias, which had been sorely ignored in both manpower and weapons over the years.

## The Capital Before Secession

The *New York Tribune* reported on April 13, 1861, that "It has long been ascertained that the game of Jefferson Davis was to strike an effective blow at some point in the South, and then move upon the Capital…with his sympathizing followers in Virginia and Maryland."

As a result, "several hundred members of volunteer companies in Washington were mustered into service for the defense of the Capital." Had the South begun the war with a march on Washington, the results could have been disastrous for the Union. Despite building its army first to prepare for war, the South was little better equipped than the North.

---

### November 6, 1860

Abraham Lincoln is elected to his first term as president.

---

## The Venomous Snakes of the South!

With rhetoric flying faster than bullets, the first days of Lincoln's administration were a verbal and administrative hell. But the situation went beyond colorful metaphors.

A mailbag sent from Virginia to Washington, DC, broke open at the postal facility days before the outbreak of the Civil War, and a box addressed to the "President of the United States" fell open. It contained two venomous snakes, which escaped and crawled free on the floor. The postal workers were incensed, as was the New York paper that reported the "deplorable example of the demoralization of the public mind in the South" and the "cowardly wretches who conceived the infamous plot."

Crew on the deck of a U.S. Navy vessel

## Not the Navy of a World Power

Estimates of the size of the U.S. Navy's fleet of warships in 1860 stood at one dozen vessels, which were fitted with a total of nearly 300 guns, almost two-thirds of which were distributed among three ships: 84 on the steam corvette *Brooklyn*, 50 on the sailing frigate *Sabine* and 40 on the steam frigate *Minnesota*. The total number of sailors, officers and men assigned to the 12 ships was estimated at just over 3000. At the same time, cargo and troop ships were busily engaged in moving both men and stores throughout the North.

Many of the vessels were chartered by the government from private companies (such as that of entrepreneur Cornelius Vanderbilt) to move troops throughout the Eastern Seaboard.

## Camp and Outpost Duty for Infantry

A simple note-book and pencil should always be carried by every officer, to issue permits, take memoranda, etc.

## Could the South Sustain War?

It was reported throughout the North that one reason war would *not* occur was because the South could not sustain it. The South had less than ample food to feed its population and could not afford to purchase more. It had no credit and no foreign or Northern supplies available to it should war be declared. The same argument was put forth regarding munitions, and it was true that the South suffered from a lack of supplies, military and otherwise, throughout the war. But confiscating U.S. government stores in the South proved to be a very successful means for launching the new army and for sustaining a war that lasted four years—when it was originally thought by both sides that the conflict would be over in four months.

**Battery:**

A group of guns in a fixed position on the battlefield or on the exterior wall of a fort. A battery typically had a number and a reference to a particular military unit or location.

# Andrew Johnson,
# Lincoln's Compromise Choice as VP

Andrew Johnson has generally been acknowledged as one of the country's worst presidents and is held up as an example of how a political decision can be more than just risky. With the war dragging on as the election of 1864 approached, when Lincoln was nominated, he chose Tennessee Democrat and senator, Andrew Johnson, as his running mate rather than vice president Hannibal Hamlin. Johnson was one of the rare Southern major office holders to stay with the Union when the Southern states seceded.

## April 15, 1861

Lincoln puts out the call: "We need to build the army and want 75,000 new volunteers."

Lincoln correctly felt that adding a Southern Democrat to his Northern Republican ticket would help garner votes, and it did. But as Lincoln prepared to end the war and begin Reconstruction, he was assassinated, leaving the lackluster vice president to take over the presidency.

Johnson was the first president to be impeached—put to the test of a vote, not actually removed from office—and he retained his office by just one thin vote.

In numerous surveys and rankings of presidents over the years, Lincoln is nearly always listed first or nearly so (at least in the top three), whereas Johnson is the opposite, always in the bottom six or eight presidents, and by some measures, he is considered possibly the worst ever. No one will ever agree on the rankings, but the consensus is clear.

## July 10, 1861

Just under three months after calling for 75,000 new troops, the face of war has changed, indeed. Lincoln asks for 500,000 more in the Union army, an increase of 567 percent more troops over the first call!

### Camp and Outpost Duty for Infantry

The men should sleep in their shirts and drawers, removing the shoes, stockings, and outer clothing, except when absolutely impracticable.

# THE FIRST SHOTS ARE FIRED

*Perhaps war was inevitable decades before; the battle over states' rights and slavery were muddied and as old as the young nation, but one thing was clear—when Lincoln was elected, the South was determined to take war to the North.*

## The First Battle

The battle for Fort Sumter was more like a spat between siblings when compared to the coming four years; it was genteel and the number of casualties was zero. It was almost the coin flip between two opposing teams—except that they were about to do battle.

The attack on Fort Sumter that started the Civil War was led by Confederate general P.G.T. Beauregard, a West Point cadet taught by Major Robert Anderson, the Union officer in the most uncomfortable of positions in April 1861. A Kentuckian, Anderson was a former slave owner and generally sympathetic to the South's political viewpoints, but a loyal Union officer, nevertheless.

Sumter was a U.S. fort on the coast and protected Charleston, South Carolina, from possible foreign attack. Anderson and his troops were effectively held hostage by the Southerners, who refused to allow supplies into the coastal fort. Then, on April 12, the stalemate ended as Anderson found himself under attack from his own countrymen— and his former Academy student. He apologized profusely to his commander-in-chief but had no choice but to surrender. He had minimal ammunition and was pinned in the fort like a cornered animal. After being battered by the Southern troops, Anderson and his men had no ammunition and no escape; even a week's ammunition would have only length-ened the one-sided encounter by a week. The Confederate army won the first "battle" of the war. It was brief, and there were no casualties, except the innocence of the young country.

## Camp and Outpost Duty for Infantry

The utmost attention will be paid by commanders of the companies to the cleanliness of the men, as to their person, clothing, arms, accoutrements, and equipment, and also as to their quarters or tents.

# Confederates Angered at Anderson's Escape to Fort Sumter

Fort Moultrie was one of three outdated and undermanned U.S. forts protecting Charleston Harbor. The commander of the small garrison there, Major Robert Anderson, continu-ally asked Washington for reinforcements or some type of assistance since war seemed imminent. He finally took mat-ters into his own hands, secretly withdrawing his men via rowboats during the night to the more heavily reinforced Fort Sumter. It was there that Anderson and his men were attacked in the battle that would start the Civil War. If not for his quick thinking, the conflict would have begun at the less-defensible Fort Moultrie and likely would have resulted in severe damage to the fort, but worse, certain substantial loss of life inside.

## The Marine Corps—Plural—North and South

The U.S. Marines have long held pride in their ranks and their accomplishments in fighting for the country. The U.S. Marine Corps was authorized to have a standing service of 4100 enlisted men at the outset of the Civil War. Even with such small numbers, it played a substantially larger role in the conflict than its Southern counterpart.

The Confederate Marine Corps was generally insignificant. It was authorized as a military branch at the beginning of the war—with a complement set at less than 1000 men: 46 officers and 944 enlisted men. That number, while almost embarrassingly low, was never attained during the war.

## Fortunately the Battle Was Delayed as Long as the Ammunition

Charles Graves, first lieutenant ordnance officer for the First Division of the Third Corps was incensed early in the war when he received an invoice (the customary paperwork always immediately preceding the arrival of supplies) for a shipment of 400,000 rounds of ball cartridges. Finally, after waiting 20 days, Graves received confirming paper-work—but never got the ammunition. It was a very familiar occurrence, with shortages in the North as well as the South, and troops were often left wondering which would come first—bullets or battle!

### Camp and Outpost Duty for Infantry

In retreat, the duties of the rear guard are of the most important nature; upon their performance the safety of the whole army depends.

# WHICH ARMY? WHAT UNIFORM? WHO'S ON FIRST?

## A Simple Case of Mistaken Identity

The well-known Army of the Potomac was, of course, Union, but the best-known Southern army was called the *Confederate* Army of the Potomac when the war began.

At the beginning of the Civil War, the two Armies of the Potomac met in battle. It was a disaster for the North. Their army was ill prepared, in men, weaponry and training. Members of Washington's high society actually went on picnics and took carriage rides between the capital and the Battle of Manassas/Bull Run. The wealthy onlookers were mortified at the butchery and death on the battlefield. After they left the area in horror, the people of the North realized how wrong they had been about the interesting little skirmish with those Southern insolents. It was not a Washington picnic; it was the start of what would be a bloody, long and difficult war.

The South renamed its Army of the Potomac the Army of Northern Virginia, and it was victorious as the early months and early battles of the war raged. But over the long, drawn-out course of the war, the Army of Northern Virginia suffered some of the highest casualties of all the Confederate forces. In fact, of the 50 units in the South that suffered the highest casualties, 40 of them were part of the Army of Northern Virginia. Of course, before passing judgment or trying to extrapolate from those numbers, you have to realize that the Army of Northern Virginia was also the largest Southern army and fought in the greatest number of and in the fiercest battles.

# Blue vs. Gray Only on the Parade Grounds

The age-old reference "Blue vs. Gray" that we all learned from television shows and history books alike was a bit of a misnomer. The Union dressed in blue and the South wearing gray uniforms has long been a popular myth. Union uniforms were certainly blue, and some Southern uniforms were gray, but two things dramatically interfered with this concept—a great many troops, far more in the South than in the North, came to war dressed in homemade uniforms because the Confederate government had no money to outfit them. The South was often referred to by Union soldiers as the army in "butternut" because of the South's beige cotton uniforms, which was a more accurate description of the color than gray.

And many units, North as well as South, outfitted themselves not just so they would have something to wear, but often with a sponsor's funds. Looking dapper was every young soldier's goal. The best example of this was the Union Zouave uniform.

For Union purposes, the Zouave was more a "what" than a "who." Originally, the term applied to Arab fighters from Morocco and Algeria who joined the French colonial army in the early 19th century. Later, French soldiers adopted the Arab dress, which consisted of brightly colored uniforms with baggy pants that were tight at the ankle, a bright sash at the waist, a short vest and jacket and a tasseled hat. Several regiments in the North adopted the Zouave uniform during the war.

After a few short weeks and a battle or two had passed, Union and Confederate soldiers only cared about staying alive and staying warm or dry, depending on the season—looks hardly mattered. A bright sash might be valuable to hold up a sagging tent, but in battles after 1861, one would be hard-pressed to find a colorful Zouave uniform among the walking—or the fallen; the baggy clothes had little chance of staying bright, clean or in one piece.

A dry uniform was the prize, and boots in one piece, with no holes in the soles, became the real treasures as time went by.

## Camp and Outpost Duty for Infantry

Soldiers will wear the prescribed uniforms in camp or garrison, and will not be permitted to keep in their possession any other clothing.

# WAR IS HELL...
# AND WORSE

## Something Worse than Gunfire?

Both sides fought under terrible conditions. Besides a shortage of rations and an equally difficult shortage of ammunition, troops had to battle diseases as well.

There was malaria from the mosquitoes and typhoid from the dirty water that troops had no choice but to drink when there was no other source available. Lice and flea infestations were common as well. In virtually every circumstance—disease, shortage of food, lack of ammunition—the difficulties were a greater problem for Southern soldiers than their Northern counterparts.

But the worst for both sides, for virtually every man in the military, were intestinal problems that affected 995 out of every 1000 soldiers (99.5 percent)—with no regard for butternut or blue! Imagine not just uncomfortable diarrhea under circumstances in battle with no sanitation, but dysentery of pandemic proportions such that thousands died from the disease. Only a rare handful somehow avoided it.

## The Union Lacked Horsepower

The Union army clearly had some holes in terms of having manpower and weapons ready for the start of the war, but it lacked horsepower as well. A cavalry does best when mounted, but even more so, soldiers weren't that willing (or that strong) when it came to pulling supply wagons themselves!

Chris Collins, the colonel commanding the 114th Pennsylvania Volunteers expressed it succinctly in 1862: "At the present moment, we have not one horse fit for work, and unless my repeated applications for teams are answered,

I shall be compelled to leave behind all my officers' tents and baggage." And they were so compelled, the officers having to abandon their gear as they marched with their men when the 114th took to the road.

## 120 Days in a Skirmish Pit

John G. Morrison, a sergeant of the 101st Illinois, spent more than four months just 300 yards from the enemy position, in a dug-out pit, with a fence, boards and tree stumps reinforcing it as his protection from the Confederates should they choose to attack. "To rise to one's feet was almost sure death from a rebel musket ball," Morrison wrote.

Morrison was part of Sherman's march to Atlanta, but earlier in the war, he was in position with the Corps of Engineers holding the line, while most of the battle was either behind him or heading toward the South.

Confederate lines, Georgia, 1864

The rebels exchanged comments, taunts and occasional musket volleys with Morrison and his men, and eventually everyone settled in to pass the time without wasting it on sarcasm and creativity. As was typically the case on quiet lines, soldiers began earnest conversation in the quiet hours. Time on the skirmish line, Morrison said, bred familiarity... and respect.

The two opposing forces began their own informal truce, and a few men from each side would walk out about 150 yards and meet in the open space between the lines to exchange news from home, the war and, most importantly, newspapers—from anywhere—with their sworn enemies who, of course, had been countrymen just a few years earlier. And as they often discovered, many were almost neighbors. In some instances, a Union soldier may have called a city home that was south of where the Confederate soldier lived. State lines were political—many soldiers in the North chose to fight for the South, and more than a few in the South felt their loyalties were in the North. More than a few instances saw battle lines drawn right through families, as well, with brothers, uncles, nephews and cousins often fighting against each other in this not-so-civil of wars.

## Camp and Outpost Duty for Infantry

The provost marshals will investigate all complaints of citizens in regard to the conduct of the troops, and will report the facts in the case to the division commander.

## Plans to Blow Up the Washington Arsenal

In November 1862, the Union army, with Confederate troops camped just two miles south of the capital, had instructions to blow up the Washington, DC, arsenal they were guarding if the Confederates moved quickly in an attempt to capture the supplies against the undermanned Union forces. Fortunately, Southern troops never mounted the anticipated "secret" assault in an attempt to obtain the stores.

### Camp and Outpost Duty for Infantry

The duties of the pickets are to keep a vigilant watch over the country in front, and over the movements of the enemy, if in sight.

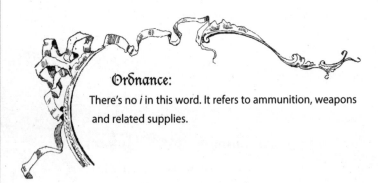

### Ordnance:

There's no *i* in this word. It refers to ammunition, weapons and related supplies.

# WHEN THE GUNS WERE SILENT

Winter quarters

## Winter "Comfort" Near Yorktown

When the winter moved in and the weather was freezing and snowing, troops hunkered down, regardless of which flag they carried. It was an undeclared truce, but neither force would march in inclement weather.

The camp that the Confederates wintering in Virginia established near Yorktown could hardly be called a resort, but they were disappointed to leave it in the spring. It was near a good stand of timber, and troops could actually build log houses insulated with scraps of wood and bits of canvas for chinking between the horizontal logs. Floors were covered with pine brush and rubber blankets.

Troops built wood stoves made of sheet and scrap iron, and some even built ovens of sundried clay bricks. The structures were cramped, with entire companies sleeping on the floor, but compared to being in holes dug in the dirt or mud somewhere else, those who could actually build winter quarters rather than simply survive in winter "locations" were by far the luckiest in the months between battles. Such a structure, with soldiers lying on top of one another on blankets, branches and dried leaves, might as well have been in a suite at the finest hotel. When spring came, the luxury was over. The marching order everyone hated to hear was "Travel light and take everything you will need. We won't be coming back."

## Camp and Outpost Duty for Infantry

One half of the officers of the pickets will always be on the alert.

## A Private Suite from a Piece of Canvas

Northern troops carried tents with them, or more accurately, half-tents. A tent wasn't complete until the soldier did some architectural design—and found a partner in a similar situation to create a home for two in the field. The Union issued rectangular fabric fitted with buttons and buttonholes that had to be attached to another soldier's identical rectangular piece of waterproof canvas to form a whole tent. The structure was then stabilized and kept upright by tying the ends to stakes in the ground, or to the butt of a rifle stuck in the ground by its bayonet.

Black soldiers in camp

⌀⌀⌀

Confederate soldiers were not issued tents or these half-tents, but instead had whatever they might have brought from home. If it was heavy, it was quickly discarded or cut down to a lightweight alternative that could be more easily carried, or the soldiers used some type of fabric to make a lean-to against a fence or other stable, upright piece of wood or even a tree.

## Camp and Outpost Duty for Infantry

Fire low. A bullet through the abdomen (belly or stomach) is more certainly fatal than if aimed at the head or heart.

As the war progressed, however, Confederate camps were dotted with Union tents "captured" in battle, which mostly meant taken from dead or wounded soldiers on the battlefield or found abandoned. The nature of this war was such that by 1865, most Confederate troops had some type of equipment, weapon, tent, haversack or canteen issued by the Union army.

The most prized captures, however, were the Union-issued, rubber-backed blankets that made the ground many times more bearable and could also be used to make a tent or lean-to to keep a soldier dry.

## Why Does that Soldier Have a Piece of Cloth Pinned to His Shirt?

Soldiers had no official identification—for example, dog tags—in the Civil War, either in the North or in the South. Many went into battle with a piece of cloth or paper pinned on their clothing with their name, unit and hometown, or with the name and address of next of kin. The odds that those tags would survive or remain whole and/or readable after a soldier was injured or killed were not good, but many were instrumental in helping medical staff identify a wounded soldier and see to it that he returned to his home and family.

And, likewise, many who were killed on the battlefield (or who died of wounds or disease in a hospital) at least received a burial at home because of the pinned badges.

But soon after the war began, creative sutlers, merchants and soldiers began fashioning the first dog tags. Some disks were produced privately and had an eagle, George Washington or Abraham Lincoln on one side, often accompanied by a patriotic slogan. The back was left blank to be engraved with a soldier's information, possibly with a list of battles in which he participated. Some disks were even made stamped with "Name," "Unit" and blank lines for the soldier to engrave himself.

Sutlers often did the engraving on site for the soldiers, so there was neither waiting nor questions about what to engrave. Still, the number of "disks," as they were called ("dog tag" was a later term), created during the Civil War was a tiny fraction of the number of soldiers—in the thousands compared to the millions of soldiers in the war.

# Civil War Castles Came Without Princesses

Hardtack. These biscuits were found after the war, preserved in this air-tight tin.

✿

The most common cuisine of combatants on both sides in the war from 1861 to 1865 was salted pork, beans—and hardtack biscuits, also known as "teeth dullers" and "worm castles," for unfortunately obvious reasons. The only royalty in these castles was small and usually in a hurry to leave the royal quarters.

The standard hardtack were simple, square, flour biscuits, and as the monikers indicate, they were baked hard and usually got stale long before they reached the soldiers. Hardtack was issued in boxes by the thousands, and, simply, it was better than nothing. Soldiers preferred to have coffee or soup in which to dunk the biscuits to soften them up a bit and save wear and tear on their teeth; it was a common and dreaded sight to dunk the cracker in liquid and a few seconds later to see the mass exodus of weevil larvae or worms emerging from the stale biscuit, adding a rather undesirable touch of protein to the cup of liquid.

## Camp and Outpost Duty for Infantry

No man shall misuse any inhabitant of the country, or take any thing by force.

### Sutler:

A sutler was a civilian merchant who sold goods to the army. Most sutlers traveled in wagons, following their units, but occasionally, near a military fort or other facility, they could operate out of an actual storefront. The wagons were amazing—they were general stores with everything a soldier might need, including canned food, pans, coffee pots, tobacco, paper, ink, pens, pencils, socks, underwear, shirts, blankets, coffee beans, matches and even dog tags. Sutlers were such a part of their units that they would accept checks or chits for what was owed them, and collect it from the unit's paymaster on payday! Many would also issue change or "good for" tokens that the men could use only at that sutler's store.

Monument on the battlefield at Bull Run, Virginia. It was the first Civil War monument erected on a battlefield and was commemorated in 1865.

cℑ℈

# Battles, Encounters, Engagements, Skirmishes and Clashes

In any war there are the major battles—the significant ones—and, unfortunately, the ones that no one has ever heard of except the families of those who died in the little, insignificant skirmishes.

## Camp and Outpost Duty for Infantry

The officer of the guard will impress upon each man the necessity of care, neatness, and soldierly bearing as sentinels.

In the Civil War, there are almost 3000 named battles, including a small number of naval encounters. They range alphabetically from Abbeville, Mississippi, to Zuni, Virginia.

We hardly would have room to list them all—that would be a small volume in itself. So with no regard for the importance, the loss of lives, the victor, the location or the dates, here are 10 battles that we've selected just on the basis of their names. They're best said aloud, which is more impressive than just reading them. Remember to precede each name with "the Battle of":

> Bird Song Ferry
> Fort Hell
> Marrowbone
> Dead Buffalo Lake
> Paint Rock River Bridge
> Hanging Rock
> Big Pigeon River
> Labadieville (also known as Thibodeauxville and
> Georgia Landing)
> Chickamicomico
> Ogeeche River Buzzard Roost Block House

Honorable mention goes to a group of battles, the first being Tongue River, accompanied by Grassy Lick, Point Lick and Salt Lick—all different battles, and with no reference to who licked whom in each!

### Kepi:

The flattened cloth hat that bears something of a resemblance to a modern baseball cap. As the war progressed, soldiers began affixing numbers or other indications of their unit to the fabric above the bill of the cap. Later in the war, the Union army began distributing insignias for the hats.

## Camp and Outpost Duty for Infantry

No person will be allowed to pass the picket line, other than general officers, and those having passes from the general commanding the division, and the general and the field officer of the day.

## The Youngest Private in Rosecrans' Camp

In April 1863, a report was sent to the headquarters of the Department of the Cumberland that read: "A flagrant outrage has been committed in your command—a person has been admitted inside your lines, without a pass, and in violation of orders…The medical director reports that an orderly sergeant in the division was today delivered of a baby, which is in violation of all military law and of the army regulations."

Experts in both statistics and humanity as involves the Civil War have never been able to provide any hard data on how many women were in the military service on either the Union or the Confederate side. Women served as spies— dressed as women as well as men—and they also worked as nurses and in other capacities in hospitals. But there are at least 20 to 30 documented cases of women masquerading

### Picket:

The soldier at the forward edge of camp standing guard to warn of any enemy troops approaching. In lulls that often lasted days or weeks, it was common for Union and Confederate pickets to chat, exchange news and act like anything but enemies.

as soldiers, undiscovered by their peers or superior officers, both for the South and the North.

This particular case, as told by a former Union captain in his memoirs in 1867, was also documented in Union records at least so far as the sergeant delivering her baby in camp.

**March 4, 1861**

Abraham Lincoln is sworn in as the nation's 16th president.

# WAR ON LAND AND SEA

*Armies and Americans on both sides realized as 1862 progressed that the war could rage for many years. When talk of secession began, war was only rhetoric, and when the war finally started, people were astonished. In the North, they thought the conflict would be brief, but not only did the rebels fight, they won. There was no end in sight, and all the talking seemed so very far away now that the dying had begun.*

## The Bloodiest Single Day of the Civil War

On September 17, 1862, the combined Union and Confederate forces suffered 23,000 casualties (dead and wounded) in the Battle of Antietam, along the creek of the same name and near the town of Sharpsburg, Maryland.

The Union and the Confederacy often had different names for battles—in this case, the conflict was known as the Battle of Antietam in the North and the Battle of Sharpsburg in the South. The North typically named the battles for landmarks and geographical features, whereas the South tended to name the battle after the closest city.

Confederate general Robert E. Lee, considered the finest general in the war, North or South, and probably the most respected soldier and gentleman by officers on both sides, led the South into battle against General George McClellan's Army of the Potomac. They fought just 40 miles from the U.S. capital. The combined forces of 100,000 men waged

> ## April 12, 1861
> War begins! The Confederates attack Fort Sumter.

IN THE HEAT OF BATTLE

a vicious, bloody battle for 14 hours before both retreated in a military draw.

The North considered it a victory, however, since it was Lee's first attempt to cut off supply lines and to move his troops into Northern territory—an action that failed. After a string of victories and positive movement, Antietam proved to be the slamming of a door, and Lee would have to find another time and route to gain a Confederate foothold in Union territory.

## The United States' First Rear Admiral

David Farragut became rear admiral in July 1862, the first officer ever to hold that rank in the U.S. Navy. The position was awarded to him in recognition of the importance of the navy to the Northern war effort.

### Camp and Outpost Duty for Infantry

Many young officers, unexpectedly taking up the profession of arms without previous experience or study, are seeking to understand their duties. The same vigilance, energy, and constant attention that give success in any pursuit in life is especially necessary here.

## Naval Advances

Although the U.S. Navy was an important part of the North's victory in the Civil War, the country's naval forces lagged behind those of other world powers. The U.S. made a concerted effort to upgrade during the war but let things lag after the war and victory. There was no significant effort to expand and upgrade the navy for several years after the conflict.

The world watched the Civil War with great interest because the U.S. had been growing into an international power while still only "fourscore and seven years" old. The development of ironclad warships prompted many countries to begin innovations on their own, realizing that the end of wooden warships was imminent.

The deck of the USS *Monitor*

## The Most Famous Naval Battle of the War

The most historic naval battle of the Civil War, or possibly of any American war, was between the former USS *Merrimac* (also spelled *Merrimack*) rebuilt as the South's CSS *Virginia*, and the North's *Monitor*. This was the world's first battle between ironclad ships, and, in a matter of hours, the age of wooden ships had passed. In the rest of the world, naval powers began planning for the change to ironclad fighting ships—virtually instantly.

## Camp and Outpost Duty for Infantry

Nothing is more certain to secure endurance and capability of long-continued effort than the avoidance of every thing as a drink except cold water (and coffee at breakfast).

Ships had been built of wood for thousands of years, but with this new design, undertaken simultaneously in the North and South, ships were now built of iron—or, at least in this era, wooden hulls were covered with iron plating—so that cannonballs would bounce off the metal instead of ripping through the wood. This change in shipbuilding technology was adopted immediately throughout the world and throughout the Union and the Confederacy as time and money would allow.

Both North and South initially claimed victory as the two ships steamed away under their own power after the battle, which took place at Hampton Roads near Chesapeake Bay on March 8, 1862. The *Virginia* was damaged, but not seriously, and withdrew to come about. The *Monitor* thought it was a withdrawal and did likewise, seemingly in victory. The *Virginia* saw this and also assumed that the opposition was withdrawing. The two ships would never have another opportunity to meet.

The actual battle began before the arrival of the much smaller *Monitor*, with the *Virginia* attacking the Union blockade off the coast. The blockade prevented foreign vessels from reaching the Confederate ports of Norfolk and Richmond to provide much-needed supplies—food, ammunition, guns and raw materials—to the South. The *Virginia* sank two Union warships and was threatening a third when the *Monitor* arrived, and the much larger, heavily weaponed *Virginia* turned to engaged her.

Casual observers of the war tend to forget that this was a *civil* war, an internal battle within a single country. Consequently, there are always debates about which soldiers were better, which general was smarter. Many in the North seem taken aback that Confederate general Lee was more highly thought of than his Union counterpart, future president Ulysses S. Grant. What is so often lost in the discussion is that they were *all* United States soldiers until 1861. They were trained, and in many cases taught, at West Point, and they were the best the country had. The only difference was that some chose the Union and others chose the Confederacy.

The *Virginia* had 10 guns ranging from 6.4 to 9 inches in diameter, plus two 12-inch howitzers and a total of 14 gun ports on both sides, as well as ports both fore and aft. The ship was also fitted with an iron ram on the bow, a device that had already proven invaluable in attacking wooden blockade ships.

The *Monitor* was a departure from the traditional naval warfare practice of fitting ships with as many guns as possible; the rule was "smaller was fine as long as quantity existed." Until this battle, naval ships were equipped with as many guns as could be fitted on deck and below decks, and warships of the era often had multiple decks with weapons on each. The *Virginia* was by far more typical, with a row of guns on each side plus a single one fore and aft. Its total number of guns was still quite low, but the guns were unusually large.

The *Monitor*, a shocking sight to anyone familiar with navy ships of the day, had just two guns on the entire ship! Both

## Camp and Outpost Duty for Infantry

Any teamster found trotting or running his team will, besides such other punishment as may be awarded him, be fined one dollar for each offense.

weapons were 11-inch guns (plans called for 15-inch ones, but they were not available in time to fit the ship, which was ready to launch and urgently needed in the war) and were mounted in a rotating turret 20 feet in diameter. The pilot-house was far forward in a small compartment on the deck, which kept the captain separated from the crew and also meant that the ship couldn't fire precisely straight over the bow.

Although both ships claimed victory, both sides suffered losses. In one sense, the Union "won" the overall battle at the site because the Confederates attacked the Union block-ade and failed to dislodge it, a critical factor in the war. On the other hand, the Union had two ships sunk and one damaged in the blockade and nearly 300 sailors killed. The Confederate navy had its ironclad damaged, but no vessels were lost and fewer than 20 Confederate sailors were killed. There was no clear victor in the ship-to-ship battle, but the North "won," keeping the blockade intact despite high losses.

The battle has been historically important to navies world-wide, ushering in a new era in naval warfare, and both the Union and Confederate navies already knew they would have to build iron ships as fast as possible for *this* war, not some far off, imagined future need.

The *Virginia* later ran aground and was burned by Southern troops to prevent it from falling into Union hands. It then exploded and was completely destroyed.

The *Monitor* had nearly as disheartening a fate. It was being towed north for repairs when it began to take on water and

## Camp and Outpost Duty for Infantry

Depredations and plundering of every description will be most surely and severely punished.

sank. Many of the crew were rescued, but 16 men on board drowned in the mishap. The ship rested on the ocean floor for 111 years before being discovered in 240 feet of water. The site was declared a National Marine Sanctuary in 1987, and major pieces of the vessel have since been raised and are on display at the Mariners' Museum in Newport News, Virginia.

## Specifications for the Combatants in the First Naval Battle Between Ironclads

|  | USS *Monitor* | USS *Merrimac*/CSS *Virginia* |
|---|---|---|
| Length | 179 feet | 278 feet |
| Beam | 49 feet | 51 feet |
| Draft | 5 feet | 21 feet |
| Speed | 8 knots | 5 to 6 knots |
| Armament | 2 11-inch guns | 2 7-inch guns<br>2 6.4-inch guns<br>6 9-inch guns<br>2 12-pound cannons |
| Complement | 58 men | 320 men |

**Monitor** ships were built immediately in the style of the Union warship the USS *Monitor* by Union shipyards and abroad. The term "monitor" was actually used worldwide from the time of the Civil War well into the 20th century. Initially, monitors were low-draft, heavily gunned and (most importantly) turreted vessels. They typically carried unusually large guns and were used to guard coasts or rivers. The key point in referring to this type of vessel as a monitor was its turreted construction and weapons capability.

## Camp and Outpost Duty for Infantry

Non-commissioned officers will, in no case, be permitted to act as waiters; nor are they, or private soldiers, not waiters, to be employed at any menial office, or made to perform any service not military, for the private benefit of any officer or mess of officers.

## Sailor from the *Monitor* Invited to Meet Lincoln

The pilot of the *Monitor*, Lieutenant John Lorimer Worden, was injured when flying particles hit him in the eyes as he steered the vessel in battle from the small pilothouse far toward the bow of the vessel. His only line of sight was out the small opening in the pilothouse, and he was hit several times with hot particles flying from the battle. He remained at his post throughout, steering the ship and maintaining strategic advantage over the *Virginia*, eventually landing the only damaging blow of the battle. Worden was evacuated to Baltimore, then taken to meet the president in Washington, DC, where Lincoln thanked him for his bravery.

## More than Drumming for the Troops

Drummer boy Orion P. Howe left his role with the 55th Illinois Volunteers to accept an appointment at the Naval School at Newport, Rhode Island (temporary location of the Naval Academy during the Civil War, because of the precarious location in Annapolis, Maryland). General Sherman made the recommendation, and President Lincoln made the appointment.

It seems that the boy didn't just drum, but was also tasked with carrying vital messages from the rear of the battle to his commanding officer on the frontlines. Despite sustaining a leg wound in battle, Howe continued on and gave the officer critical information regarding vital ammunition needs for the troops. Without the information, or if the wrong information had been passed along because the boy misheard or misspoke, the company could have ended up facing the enemy with empty guns. Howe, in this case, made the officer in charge aware of the situation, telling him that there was urgent need for more ammunition and that it was an unusual caliber (.54) for which they were waiting.

> ## Camp and Outpost Duty for Infantry
>
> Special care shall be taken to ascertain that no ball-cartridges are mixed with the blank cartridges issued to the men.

## Who Was that Masked Man?

By far the best-known name among photographers of the era was Mathew Brady, who was already an established studio photographer in Washington, DC, when the war broke out. If Lincoln wanted a sitting, he went to Brady; if Brady wanted a portrait of the president, Lincoln obliged. He was clearly the single most dominant photographer of the time and immediately went out into the field to chronicle the historic event.

Brady's name was and still remains synonymous with photography during the Civil War, but it was actually his assistants who handled much of the fieldwork as the war progressed, because Brady, unbeknownst to anyone, was losing his sight.

There were a great many photographers in the field chronicling the war, but the vast majority lacked Brady's—and his staff's—skills. And in studios from Harrisburg to New Orleans, an entire new industry cropped up—production of the portraits of officers, enlisted men and their families. Soldiers often posed with their weapons, or with those provided at the studio, so the fighting men (many who had yet to report to their units) might be shown with a pistol or two, a rifle with bayonet and one or two Bowie knives. Literally, hundreds of thousands of prints were made and to this day can be found in private and museum collections sorted by subject, state, gender, unit and rank. As one might guess, the scarcity of some subjects makes photos of them highly valuable, whereas prints of common, unknown soldiers are worth much less, and photos of the most mundane subjects are even less expensive. Larger-format prints and glass negatives command much higher prices, and auction values in Civil War photography collecting can range from $25 to hundreds of thousands of dollars per print.

Samples of Confederate currency

## Inflation in the South

Confederate dollars bought less and less as the war went on, and at one point, chickens cost $50 each and butter was

$20 per pound. But the women of the South remained unwavering. They claimed their faith was two-fold—they believed in God and in General Robert E. Lee.

## Worthless Paper

It was said during the waning days of the war, when Richmond was suffering horrible inflation, that you went to the market with your currency in a basket and came home with your purchases in your wallet.

### Camp and Outpost Duty for Infantry

It is frequently more necessary to prevent a person going out than coming in, for the reason that a single party (however loyal, if captured) getting out, may give information to the enemy of the location of our troops.

## One Union Officer's Impression of the South

A Union officer, moving into the South with his troops, included in his report of his command a note on the Confederate States: "I find there are two classes of white people in this country, the rich and the poor. And the poor are happy to say where stores are held and to help us. They aren't slaveholders and they aren't supportive of the Confederacy."

## A Medal Honoring the Defenders of Fort Sumter

While there was a U.S. Government medal issued to each of the men at Fort Sumter, honoring them for their bravery and perseverance in the face of the attack, another medal was issued to commemorate the event. The privately issued, 34-mm medal was engraved by George Lovett Sr., one of the best-known medalists of the time. The medal was created in 1861 in brass, copper and a white alloy. It remains unknown today for whom Lovett made the medal and how it was distributed. It is quite rare and was apparently minted in very small numbers. The medal reads: "Fort Sumter was evacuated with all the honors of war after a most heroic defense by Maj. R. Anderson, with a garrison of 75 men against a terrific bombardment of 30 hours duration by the So. Ca. Rebels numbering 8100."

## The Number One Item in Camp

No debate. The most important item in any camp was coffee. The more desperate the soldiers got, the more creative they became, making a drink from chicory root, almost any berry or anything else that was handy. But when coffee beans were available, typically far more often in the North than the South, they were distributed to the men.

Few soldiers had the luxury of more than a tin drinking cup, and when there wasn't a mess tent, that tin cup became a cooking pot, serving dish and coffee pot, too. Often the men would use the thick end of a bayonet to "grind" the beans, then pour heated water over them in the cup. The beans were often green, but as long as *any* coffee beans were available, complaints were minimal.

Students of the Civil War have studied Lincoln's appearance from his early debates for the Senate seat won by Stephen Douglas, to his presidential campaign and election of 1860 through to the war years of 1861 to 1865. As time went on, the lines in Lincoln's face grew deeper and harder, and his skin, like his demeanor, seemed to weather and take on the pain of every battle. He grew more tired but more resolved; he said less but demanded more. At one point, while discussing possible terms of Confederate surrender (which turned out to be many months distant), he told his generals he wanted one thing and one thing immediately—to "bring our boys home!"

# JUST TOO MANY WAYS TO DIE!

## They Always Say that Running Away Solves Nothing!

The strict penalty for desertion during the Civil War was execution, but there was an applied policy of leniency in one particular course of action or case of desertion—when a soldier immediately returned to rectify the situation.

If the deserter or deserters immediately rejoined their regiment and took up arms against the enemy, the charges were often dropped or never even filed—and officially forgotten. Needless to say, if a man was on the run, resisted being taken back and refused to rejoin his unit, being caught was a very bad idea. It nearly always meant a quick death by firing squad.

In more complicated cases of desertion, for example, when a man went over to the opposing side, committed other crimes or attacked or injured a fellow soldier, he was also destined for the firing squad in most cases. Occasionally, a trial might save his life. It was not uncommon to have a deserter join the enemy only to be wounded or killed in combat. For the myriad circumstances, it seemed there were myriad possible outcomes.

A common practice discussed by soldiers, especially those who had firsthand knowledge, was the practice of a hasty

### Camp and Outpost Duty for Infantry

Any person approaching the sentinels at night must be challenged in a loud tone and commanded to halt. Refusing to halt, the sentinel is to fire.

execution in the field. There was no waiting for a trial, taking a prisoner to headquarters or delaying the outcome.

Some "standard practices" were written about and actually captured by camp-following photographers during the war. Once the deserter was recaptured and the commanding officer had passed sentence, the regiment was gathered in formation to witness the prisoner—and a coffin—brought forward. Soldiers faced the prisoner or formed three sides of a square with the soldier standing behind or kneeling on his coffin in the open side of the formation.

A firing squad of 10 men was selected—nine with live ammunition in their rifles and one without, so that no soldier could be certain if he killed the deserter.

The worst job of the assembled troops was given to a single soldier, who was armed with a pistol and given the duty, if the nine bullets somehow failed to kill the deserter, of putting a bullet in the doomed man's head immediately so he would not suffer.

One soldier told the story of watching an execution, shaking while holding his pistol—and having his greatest fear come to pass. "Oh, God! Oh, God! I'm dead!" shouted the wounded deserter, writhing on the ground. Before the soldier could aim the pistol with his shaking hand, his friend—the deserter—grew quiet and died.

During the war, about 300 deserters were executed—roughly the same number who died of sunstroke during the conflict.

## Camp and Outpost Duty for Infantry

Better to fire only one shot in five minutes, and that carefully, than ten in one minute without aiming at all.

Cemetery at Alexandria, Virginia

## 600,000 Total Dead in the War

It's virtually impossible for us to imagine more than a half million dead people; envisioning acres of a battlefield strewn with 10,000 bodies is impossible in itself.

Try to picture 600,000, not as numbers on a page, but as human beings in front of or all around you in terms you can more easily visualize:

☞ Imagine 40,000 elevators, each filled with 15 people, in office buildings throughout the downtown core.

☞ Or picture not just one packed baseball stadium on a summer night, but 15 major league stadiums seating 40,000 each—with every seat taken.

☞ Can't find a seat in the new 300-seat multiplex theater? If the fancy building has 10 screens, that's 3000 folks when every theater is totally full, but you would need 200 complexes of 10 theaters each!

- ☞ What about that super new gym with rows of bikes, stair climbers, treadmills and more? If 600,000 people were exercising, you'd need about 10,000 gyms!

- ☞ How large would a parking garage need to be to hold all those people? Imagine sedans, each with four people inside, and compact cars with just one or two passengers. Better find more than 100 garages because you'll need about 240,000 cars to hold them all.

- ☞ Sorry, no aisle seats for you on that Boeing 737 aircraft, which only holds 150 weary travelers. You'll need 4000 planes.

- ☞ Have you ever been to a totally sold-out college or NFL game? Do you remember what 60,000-plus fans look like? Picture 10 stadiums side by side—that's 600,000 fans—the population of Seattle or Denver or Nashville or Milwaukee or Washington, DC—and every single person in any one of those cities…dead.

Any one of these represents 600,000 Civil War dead.

## How Fast Can War Kill?

In June 1864, in an artillery charge at Petersburg, Virginia, the 1st Maine Artillery lost 635 of its 900 men—in seven minutes of action. That is 70.55 percent of its men in just seven minutes, more than 10 percent of its total complement of soldiers each minute, and 1.5 men every second!

### Camp and Outpost Duty for Infantry

In the bivouac, shelter should be provided for the animals if possible. They should not stand in low, damp, or wet ground.

General Robert E. Lee's headquarters at Gettysburg

## The Bloodiest Time in the United States

In a span of just five months in the middle of the war, three battles set the stage for the final outcome, for the North to turn back the invading Confederate army. These months were the most costly in terms of total American lives—Union and Confederate—combined. Until then, the Confederates had been winning battles and were holding their own against the larger, stronger North.

At Chancellorsville, in a battle that lasted from May 1 to 4, 1863, perhaps the single most important event to affect the South occurred and may well have cost them the victory. General Stonewall Jackson, acknowledged to be the greatest strategist among all the generals, North and South, was shot accidentally by his own troops—they mistook him for an enemy soldier—and died from his wounds shortly thereafter. It was the greatest single loss at Chancellorsville or in any other conflict. In that battle, the North had 134,000 troops compared to just 60,000 in Lee's Southern army. Lee suffered 13,000 casualties and Joseph Hooker's Union army lost 17,000, and despite having almost 75,000 fewer troops, Lee prevailed.

Two months later, from July 1 to 3, 1863, a battle took place in Gettysburg that is acknowledged as the event that truly changed the course of the war. The South was pushing into the North, and General Lee was planning to march through Pennsylvania toward the nation's capital after the battle at Gettysburg, which he fully expected to win. If Jackson had been there with Lee, the Confederate army might well have succeeded.

At Gettysburg, more than 150,000 total troops were engaged and a full one-third of all of them were either killed or wounded. Lee also lost an inordinately high number of his commanders on the heels of losing his finest general, leaving him very short on experienced commanding officers for the rest of the war.

As the huge numbers of troops entered Gettysburg and the surrounding fields, they literally stretched beyond anyone's field of vision. General Sedgwick's corps consisted of 18,000 men, whom he had marched for more than 18 hours to reach the city, the line stretching out of sight 10 miles down the dirt road.

The number of casualties was so staggering on both sides that it became almost impossible simply to judge battles by

## Camp and Outpost Duty for Infantry

No soldiers shall ride in loaded baggage-wagons, under any circumstances, nor in empty wagons, unless by special instructions to that effect.

statistical information and losses. At Gettysburg, one company began with only 84 men (a standard company was 100 men, but as the war went on, numbers would continually shrink until new recruits could be added), but every single one was either wounded or killed during the battle. The 26th North Carolina Infantry went into battle at Gettysburg with 800 men; three days later, 708 were dead, wounded or missing.

Then, two months later, 58,000 Union troops under the command of William Rosecrans engaged Braxton Bragg's 66,000 Confederate troops, a rare manpower advantage for the South at the battle of Chickamauga, Georgia, on September 19 and 20. Bragg suffered 18,000 casualties, the North 16,000, and the Confederates were victorious. However, it only forestalled the inevitable defeats throughout the South, while the battle at Gettysburg resulted in pushing back the Confederates in the North.

Those three battles in less than five months saw a combined total of North and South casualties of 114,000 men!

## Camp and Outpost Duty for Infantry

When an officer or soldier deserves mention for conduct in action, a special report shall be made in his case, and the general commander-in-chief decides whether to mention him in his report to the government and in his orders.

## Civil War Torpedoes

Approximately 50 vessels (in both Union and Confederate navies) were sunk by torpedoes during the Civil War. The Confederates planted 123 torpedoes in Charleston Harbor to prevent Northern vessels from entering. But how do you plant a torpedo? Aren't they very long and skinny like a big, giant cigar, fired from a submarine or possibly from a surface ship at an enemy ship?

Not in the Civil War. The term "torpedo" as used in the war made reference to a round, anchored explosive floating below the surface of the water, which would explode on contact with the hull of a ship. Any good World War II movie will provide ample visuals on how harbors were filled with these mines to thwart enemy ships from entering. During the Civil War, torpedoes were anchored to the sea bottom in the hope that an enemy ship would hit the floating bomb and trigger it with its hull.

The torpedoes, a crude version of the round floating mines of the 20th century, were made in various shapes and sizes, the key being that 1) they would float, and 2) they would keep their explosive charge dry. Sometimes, they were anchored to the bottom, but in other cases, they were anchored to multiple spots along the sloping shoreline and the bottom, forming a "spider web" connected to floats. When a ship came through the area, it would snag on the connecting lines and ignite the explosives. Other torpedoes were actually ignited from a manned station onshore when a ship was sighted by the shore guards.

## Camp and Outpost Duty for Infantry

The ambulance depot, to which the wounded are carried or directed for immediate treatment, is generally established at the most convenient building nearest the field of battle. A red flag marks its place, or the way to it.

IN THE HEAT OF BATTLE

"**Damn** the torpedoes! Full speed ahead!" David Farragut, Civil War admiral of the Union naval forces and the first American officer to hold the title of admiral, is famous for two things: the above quote and being appointed the United States' first admiral.

The U.S. Navy had resisted the use of the rank "admiral" for no other reason than to differentiate itself from European navies, where such a title was common for the highest-ranking officers.

Farragut, born in the South and married to a Southern woman, made it clear to everyone with whom he spoke before the war started that he believed anyone seceding was a traitor. Still, he had to prove himself to the Union, which he did. He was also an annoyance on occasion, making arbitrary decisions that would cause a coordinated attack with land troops to have to be postponed, or worse, simply to fail.

But, in a crucial battle, the U.S. Navy fleet was set to withdraw from the siege of Mobile, a vital port that Farragut desperately wanted to capture. He was commanding not just from the flag vessel of the force, but was as high up as he could get in order to see what was happening. He was lashed to the rigging of the USS *Hartford* when he uttered his famous "Damn the torpedoes!" quote and bore down on Mobile Bay, ultimately defeating the Confederate troops and the gun emplacements there.

The net result of Farragut's presence was a continued growth of the U.S. Navy as a power. With the construction of ironclads and the defeat of the Confederacy, the war was certainly a factor in the development of the United States Navy.

Federal battery at the siege of Yorktown, Virginia

⚜

# Heavyweight Weaponry

Artillery shells in the Civil War were measured by one of two distinct references, inches or pounds. The inches measured the diameter of the bore (the inside of the barrel of the gun), while the weight, which referred to the size of the shells, could be a very confusing and not-as-it-seemed measure. The weight often fluctuated, because one measurement would be picked up from its original, accurate reference and be used to refer to different munitions later on. For example, the term "12-pounder" obviously originated with a shell or ball weighing 12 pounds. A 12-pound shell was fired from a 4.62-inch bore, so later, whatever was fired from a 4.62-inch bore was called a 12-pounder because that was far simpler than saying "a four-point-six-two-incher."

So a 12-pounder was essentially a round cannonball that weighed 12 pounds *or* it was a conical shell that at one time weighed 12 pounds but now might not, but would fit in a 4.62-inch shell. Simple enough?

One very simple fact was that any soldier who was hit by a 12-pound ball or a roughly 12-pound conical shell would cease to exist. There would be little worry about torn flesh or other injuries—there would simply be no more soldier.

Those who fought in the war told unbelievable stories of looking down the line and seeing fellow soldiers "liquefied" before their eyes. They simply vanished or, after the horrible squeal of an artillery shot flying through the line, there would simply be ooze and liquid on the ground surrounded by pieces of fabric and weapons—all that remained of friends and comrades.

Some of the largest artillery guns used in the Civil War included the big 12-pounders and the smaller-bore (2.9- to 3.0-inch) 10-pounders. There were also even larger guns that were kept relatively stationary because of their weight and the difficulty moving them, such as the 24-pound howitzer with a 5.82-inch bore. The value in a given situation would be dependent on the size of the projectile that could be fired, the range of the enemy and the overall weight of the gun and wagon together, as well as the speed with which it could be relocated to adjust to moving enemy troops. These weapons had a range of 1000 to nearly 3000 yards—more than a half-mile to nearly two miles—and, unbelievably, the projectiles traveled at a velocity of about 1200 feet per second, or 800-plus miles per hour. Again, forgetting the statistics, from a mile away, a deadly projectile fired from a 12-pounder would take all of four and a half seconds to crash into the enemy. That's roughly the speed of sound. So when the soldiers heard the huge explosion of the enemy cannon being fired, the ball or shrapnel or other killing pieces of metal would be just about

Confederate soldiers with howitzers, Richmond, Virginia

ripping into their line of infantrymen. Besides cannonballs and shells, canisters and round containers filled with shot (like a shotgun shell) were also used and could be even more deadly as anti-infantry weapons. A canister filled with shrapnel or steel balls could effectively rip soldiers to shreds.

## Camp and Outpost Duty for Infantry

Wagons will assemble at the left of the line of tents or bivouacs, under charge of the quarter-master. The regimental quarter-master will then report to the brigade quarter-master that his train is ready, and ask for instructions.

# TRULY AN INTERNATIONAL WAR

## Far-reaching Battles from New Mexico to Texas…to France?

In 1864, the USS *Kearsarge* and the CSS *Alabama* fought an hour-long naval battle that resulted in the sinking of the *Alabama*. The Union ship had chased the Confederate ship halfway around the world, and the battle was fought in the English Channel and watched by Frenchmen standing on the shore.

But, amazingly, that was not the only international naval encounter of the Civil War. Another Confederate ship, the cruiser *Shenandoah*, actually completely circumnavigated the globe, harassing Union shipping wherever possible. The *Shenandoah* finally surrendered to the British at Liverpool, a full seven months after the war ended.

### Battles Took Place Far and Wide

The Federal Adjutant General's Office lists almost 3000 registered "official" battles in the Civil War, about 100 of which were naval battles. And, not limited to the United *States*, conflicts also took place in U.S. territories—the Indian Territories, Arizona Territory, Dakota Territory and Utah Territory.

### The United States vs. the World

While the U.S. was at war with itself, losing men by the tens of thousands in battles, what might have happened if an international conflict began? The U.S. was only worried about France's aid to the Confederates, and the Confederates likewise saw the English helping their former colonies. There was no serious threat of a third party entering the conflict,

but there were formidable armies abroad. In 1864, a report
was issued citing the size of European armies and the percentage of countries' national budgets spent on their military:

| Country | Military strength | Percentage of annual budget |
|---|---|---|
| Russia | 1,000,000 men | 42 percent |
| France | 573,000 men | 34 percent |
| Austria | 467,000 men | 37 percent |
| Turkey | 424,000 men | unknown |
| Italy | 314,000 men | unknown |
| England | 300,000 men | 39 percent |
| Prussia | 124,000 men | 30 percent |
| Sweden | 67,000 men | 40 percent |
| Denmark | 50,000 men | 37 percent |

## Camp and Outpost Duty for Infantry

Loose bowels, namely, acting more than once a day,
with a feeling of debility afterward, is the first step
toward cholera; the best remedy is instant and perfect
quietude of the body, eating nothing but boiled rice
with or without boiled milk.

# Neither Able nor Agile

Colonel Abel Smith, commander of the 13th regiment of the
New York Militia, came home to visit his family and escort
new recruits of the regiment to a bivouac in Brooklyn.

Upon reboarding the train that was in motion as it left Mechanicsville, New York, his foot slipped and he landed on the rails. Everyone watching was horrified, then they seemed to give a cumulative sigh of relief as the colonel sat up and announced he was just fine. But as those around tried to help him to his feet, he discovered that both legs were broken, as was his shoulder and arm. He lapsed into unconsciousness before he could be taken to a nearby hotel and died within hours.

# Oregon Loses a Senator

Oregon, which became a state in 1859, ceding a good part of the Northwest to the new Washington Territory, had Edward Baker, who was well-known in the military for his heroism in the Mexican War, as a senator. He was formerly a Congressman from Illinois, and when the Civil War began just two years after Oregon achieved statehood, Baker formed the California Volunteers and took the rank of colonel. Although he refused the rank of general at the time, he was a general when he was killed at the Battle of Ball's Bluff near Leesburg, Virginia, on October 21, 1861.

### Far-flung War Reached New Mexico in Early 1862

The first reports of battle in New Mexico came from Fort Craig. Confederate troops, made up primarily of men from Texas, approached the fort with 1500 cavalry troops, 500 to the rear in reserve and six pieces of artillery. The Union forces repelled the first attack and captured 100 of the enemy, but, unfortunately, the 100 were all mules and not soldiers. They also captured the wagonmaster and killed "a great number" of Texans, according to their report.

### Citizens Are Asked to Turn in Their Firearms

Early in the war, the *New York Times* reported that President Lincoln had asked private citizens in Richmond, the seat of the Confederacy, to turn in their firearms and to remain uninvolved in the hostilities. Astonishingly, they obeyed. Shotguns were excluded, but the government (Union!) reported accepting 7000 guns, as well as 200 sabers and 70 artillery swords.

Beyond amazing.

## Camp and Outpost Duty for Infantry

The commandant of the grand guard will pass along each picket-guard, to see that the officers have properly instructed their men.

## The Cargo Was in Good Shape, But What About the Crew?

A private vessel carrying goods to New York during the war was announced in the *New York Times* as "Ship *London* arrived NY, 8 days of gales and heavy seas. Chas. Becher lost, fell from jib boom. James Richmond died en route from disease and exposure."

The report was not unusual in the mid-19th century; a death or two on a transatlantic crossing was, unfortunately, quite the norm. With no complaints, no corrections and no reason to think otherwise, the crossing and the docking in New York would be logged and done. But in this case, a crewman with a badly bruised and mangled arm went directly to the harbormaster to report more than irregularities. He said that the first and second mates had severely beaten him and several crewmembers, including Becher and Richmond. When the New York authorities began to investigate, they found that both mates had disappeared when the ship docked. Becher did fall from the boom, where he had climbed to escape, and Richmond's only illness was blood loss from beatings. Four other crewmen were hospitalized with wounds so severe as to be permanently disabling. Just another Civil War cargo crossing.

**Blockade (Naval):**
Ships positioned close to shore along a coastline near a harbor to block enemy shipping or ships friendly to the enemy bringing supplies to the port. The Union navy, with its superior numbers, successfully blockaded many Southern ports, in what was strategically one of the most important actions of the Union, other than actual battle.

## 19th-century Super Tanker

The ship *Elvira Owen* left Philadelphia in 1865 for Antwerp carrying 198,683 gallons of refined and 89,392 gallons of crude petroleum, the cargo valued at $155,221. Almost 300,000 gallons is a very large load of petroleum in any century!

### A Good Haul in Tennessee

Following a small skirmish in Charlestown, Tennessee, General Braxton Bragg reported that his men captured "700 prisoners, 50 wagons loaded with stores, 10 ambulances, 6 pieces of artillery, a lot of horses, mules and other property."

### March 9, 1862
The *Monitor* takes on the *Virginia* at Hampton Roads.

## Red Water

When someone said that the creeks ran red at Gettysburg and other battles, it was neither poetic nor an exaggeration. The killing or wounding of literally hundreds of men standing in or near a section of a stream turned the shallow water from clear to various shades of red.

### Camp and Outpost Duty for Infantry

The sentinels are not to judge the passes. This must always be done by an officer.

# THE GENERALS

## Philip Sheridan (1831–88), Union

Sheridan, a general in the Union army, was despised by Southerners for his policy of torching any and all property in his path. Whenever his troops were victorious in battle, he would have his men burn whatever was in the way en route to the next conflict.

The South was desperate for food during the war, and the grains and other crops that were grown were always inadequate for the needs of the Confederates. Just as the naval blockades were intended to keep valuable supplies and weapons from reaching the Confederate army, Sheridan knew that every acre he burned would bring the South closer to defeat. His policy obviously instilled hatred in the enemy. Confederate women, children and men all hated Sheridan as well.

By the time Sheridan had been through the picturesque Shenandoah Valley, Confederate troops were left in shambles, and one of the most beautiful areas of the South—of the entire country—was a charred ruin.

It wasn't avarice that drove Sheridan's actions; it was Grant's orders. Sheridan had been ordered to do everything possible to stop the Rebel troops and to deprive them of anything that would help continue the war—livestock, wheat, barley, timber and captured weapons.

## Ulysses S. Grant (1822–85), Union

Grant was an intelligent, driven and pragmatic general in charge of all the armies of the North. He was also saddled with a mostly accurate reputation for excessive drinking. That he was subsequently elected as president of the United States speaks clearly to what the majority of Americans felt about him after the conflict.

Grant was well known for his drive, and, after a victory over Southern forces, when he was asked for terms, he responded that the only acceptable terms would be unconditional surrender. His response summed up with clarity how he fought the entire war.

Early in the war, the consensus—and accurately so—was that the better leaders of the military were in the South. It was no secret that Robert E. Lee was considered the finest general in the United States prior to 1861, but he chose to represent his home state of Virginia rather than the Union in the war. Such choices were perhaps indicative that something more than slavery issues were the catalyst for the conflict. The choices that people such as Lee made expressed not only feelings about states' rights, but, even more so, loyalty to one's homeland—the home *state*—especially in the South. In the North, from New York to Massachusetts to New Hampshire, there was a pride and loyalty to the *Union*; in the South, conversely, loyalties were to the places called *home*. And Lee was a Virginian. For the first part of the war, he and his generals proved that their skills were generally finer than those of their Northern counterparts. Even Lincoln felt this to be the case. It wasn't until there were substantial victories by Grant-led forces that Lincoln recognized his general as Lee's equal and promoted him to the rank of major general.

At West Point, Grant was not obscure, but neither was he outstanding. After graduating in the middle of his class, he enlisted in the infantry and went to war against Mexico, where his general, Zachary Taylor, cited him for vigor and tenacity. Grant was steadfast in getting the job done both then and in the Civil War. He was later promoted from major general to general-in-chief in the final year of the war.

It was Grant who meticulously worded the terms of Lee's surrender at Appomattox to ensure the dignity of the defeated

## Camp and Outpost Duty for Infantry

Deserters from the enemy, after being examined, will be secured for some days, as they may be spies in disguise.

troops and also to guarantee that they would not face any treason charges after the fact.

First elected in 1868 and then reelected in 1872 for a second term as president, Grant, known for his incorruptibility, was continually embroiled in political problems. These issues continued to haunt him in private business after he completed his two terms as president. He was mired in severe financial problems and facing terminal throat cancer, but forced himself through sheer will to finish writing his memoirs to ensure that his family would have adequate money on which to live. It was Mark Twain who financed and engineered the publication of the hugely successful two-volume work. Grant lived only long enough to know that the project would succeed, as he died literally hours after he finished writing. There were rumors that Twain actually wrote the memoirs or polished them for Grant, but they were just that—rumors.

## Rank and File

Did you know that there were six ranks of general in the Union army? In order from highest rank to lowest, they were as follows:

- General-in-Chief
- General of the Army
- General
- Lieutenant General
- Major General
- Brigadier General

And moving down the list, the ranks were as follows:

- Colonel
- Lieutenant Colonel
- Major
- Captain
- First Lieutenant
- Second Lieutenant

# George Armstrong Custer (1839–76), Union

Custer, a general in the Union army, was just 26 years old at the end of the Civil War. It is difficult to separate the man from his legend and his folly after the war to ascertain just how history might have judged him on his Civil War performance alone.

His arrogance and stupidity in defeat at the hands of Native Americans at the Battle of the Little Bighorn River will forever colour our perception of Custer. For nearly a century after the battle in Montana, the event was known for the massacre of American troops. Custer and U.S. Army leaders were considered heroes of the West for protecting settlers who *had* to be right because they were, after all, "white and Americans." Finally, by the middle of the 20th century, Custer and men like him (though he was worse than most—than any—in his treatment of and hostility toward the American Indians) were being vilified and held up to ridicule for their treatment of the Native Americans, who were, after all, the ones massacred in most cases. Had all this not been part of his history, what might George Custer have achieved—perhaps only more disgrace—had he not died well before his 40th birthday?

Born in 1839, Custer graduated from West Point just as the Civil War was beginning. He was last in his class as a cadet, and without the war on the horizon, he may never have been given a commission in the army.

Early on, Custer earned a reputation for bravery and tenacity—and flamboyance. At 23, he was the army's youngest general, and after the Civil War, he remained in the army and began to make the West his personal shooting gallery. With the government's policy of manifest destiny and no more than lip service paid to Native American rights, Custer was a "successful Indian fighter" for several years and was known, and hated, by various Indian nations.

It was more fitting than ironic that Custer led his men into a massacre at Little Big Horn because it was his own arrogance and misreading of the situation, as well as the size of the Cheyenne encampment and fighting force, that led to the death of his troops. Custer and his men realized just moments before they went into battle that they were not just outnumbered, but also completely surrounded and trapped with no way to escape. It took just minutes for the Native American warriors to encircle and kill every man in the unit, including their commander, 36-year-old George Armstrong Custer.

Many look at Custer's successes in the Civil War as those of a very young, aggressive and overconfident leader. Then they examine his defeat at Little Big Horn and realize that perhaps the only difference in outcomes between the two was that Custer was simply luckier in the Civil War. His arrogance later caught up to him, but white Americans have always been fascinated with his exploits as an "Indian fighter," for decades idolizing his martyrdom and then ridiculing the stupidity that cost the life of every soldier with him that day.

Character studies in American film over the years remain an interesting interpretive saga of Custer and the Little Big Horn. As with many other heroes and villains of 19th-century Civil War and western history, we remain fascinated by the fighters and their stories, and always at the top of that list is the enigmatic Custer.

## Camp and Outpost Duty for Infantry

It is better to avoid villages; but if the route lies through them, officers and non-commissioned officers are to be vigilant to preventing straggling.

## Abner Doubleday (1819–93), Union

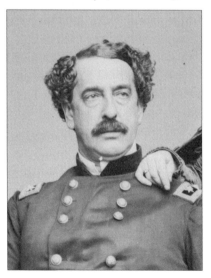

Regarded as a fiercely loyal and anti-slavery general in the Union army, Doubleday's greatest fame, beyond his army and business careers, is that, despite virtually every historical bit of evidence to the contrary, he has been credited as the man who invented baseball!

The story points to Doubleday as a young man in 1839 in the small town of Cooperstown, New York, inventing the rules of baseball and the veritable basics of how the game should be played. However, according to all the records, the then-20-year-old Doubleday was a cadet at West Point and spent all his time there in 1839.

Even though a letter from one person (just one!), who was a very young child in Cooperstown in 1839 and wrote the letter later in life, describes how Doubleday created America's pastime, no one has *ever* found proof of precisely how the game was invented or that Doubleday had anything to do with its creation.

In 1939, that same small New York village, Cooperstown—founded by author James Fennimore Cooper's father—became the modern home to the new Baseball Hall of Fame. The stadium there is Doubleday Field, and for *no* reason but blind sentimentality, the location of the Hall of Fame, the construction of a wonderful, small ballpark and at least a bit of the allure and alleged history of baseball is linked to General Doubleday and the cozy little town named for James Fennimore Cooper's dad.

During the Civil War, the name of Abner Doubleday was in the headlines from the absolute beginning. No youngster in military terms when the war began, he was at Fort Sumter in 1861, 41 years old, a veteran of the Mexican and Seminole

## Camp and Outpost Duty for Infantry

The order of the baggage will be as follows, unless otherwise directed: 1st, ammunition; 2d, hospital baggage; 3d, cooking utensils, and cooked or small rations; last, other baggage.

wars, and an artillery captain. Throughout the war, he proved his worth and often was put in less-than-advantageous positions, regrouping after the loss of a commanding officer, outnumbered by his Confederate opposition and, in more than one case, involved in political infighting in the army with General Meade, who replaced Doubleday when inadvertently given false information about his performance at Gettysburg. But Meade already disliked Doubleday and felt he was indecisive. Later, his command stripped, Doubleday was assigned to the proverbial "desk job" in Washington and took the opportunity to testify before a committee on the conduct of the war, strongly criticizing Meade for his performance at Gettysburg.

Doubleday remained in the army after the war. He held such posts as recruiting director in San Francisco (where he patented a cable car system and operated the first of the city's famous cable car lines!) and commander of a unit of black soldiers in Texas.

General Abner Doubleday swore he had nothing to do with the origins of the game, and, until the day he died in 1893, he was still attempting to refute the stories about his invention of the game of baseball. All historical research corroborates that point, but the general's memory will always be saddled with that historical footnote. Fortunately, it is not a negative one, just an incorrect basis for his ongoing adulation.

## Camp and Outpost Duty for Infantry

The following should be reported to the adjutant general of the Army: recruiting return, monthly; quarterly return of deceased soldiers; annual return of casualties and immediately change of staff officers and receipt of blankets, etc.

# William Tecumseh Sherman (1820–91), Union

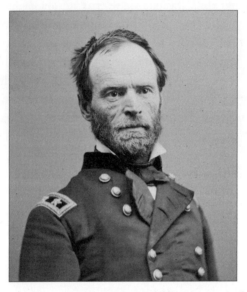

Sherman is well known among Civil War generals for having one of the "best" names and one of the better scowls to go with it. Apparently "Tecumseh" came from what he said was his father's appreciation of the Shawnee Indians at one point in his life.

Sherman was known as a strong tactical leader, but also as the man who burned everything in his path during his famous March to the Sea after capturing Atlanta and with Civil War victory imminent.

The Union army was shocked, perhaps not quite as much as the citizenry, at its defeats early in the war at the hands of the supposedly undermanned, undersupplied and underfinanced Confederate army. The Southern troops were all that, but the Union grossly underestimated the "fight" in the fighters, and at the First Battle of Bull Run, in which the South defeated the North badly, one bright spot that Lincoln saw was Sherman's skilled leadership; this resulted in his promotion to general that same year.

When Sherman first heard that the Confederacy was becoming a reality with the secession by South Carolina, he sent a note to a good friend in disbelief. Sherman's letter was an eerie portent of what was to come:

> *You people of the South don't know what you are doing. This country will be drenched in blood, and God only knows how it will end....You mistake the people of the North. They are not going to let this country be destroyed without a mighty effort to save it....The North can make a steam engine, locomotive or railway car; hardly a yard of cloth or pair of shoes can you make. At first you will make headway, but as your limited resources begin to fail, shut out from the markets of Europe as you will be, your cause will begin to wane.*

Together with Grant, Sherman was able to salvage something out of the Battle of Shiloh when a devastating defeat seemed imminent. Although others undoubtedly also said it, Sherman has been credited for coining the phrase "War is hell" in a speech at West Point years after the Civil War, and indeed it was and still is.

## Camp and Outpost Duty for Infantry

The quarter-master should give special attention to the ambulances; see that they are always in good order, the litters working easily and freely—never, under any circumstances, permitting drivers others to use them as beds or to sleep in them. *Whoever has so little regard for the comfort of a wounded soldier as to allow the ambulance provided for his comfort to be used, or to be neglected, should be most severely punished.*

There were over 400 Confederate generals throughout the war, including Robert E. Lee, Thomas "Stonewall" Jackson and James Longstreet. Jackson was eventually killed by his own men, who mistook him for the enemy.

The Union army had more than 550 generals, including Ulysses S. Grant, Phil Sheridan, William Tecumseh Sherman, Dan Sickles and George Armstrong Custer. General Sickles had his leg amputated after it was crushed by a cannonball at the Battle of Gettysburg. He kept the amputated leg bone and the cannonball, and later presented both to the Army Medical Museum.

One person who was not promoted to general was a Polish immigrant named Wladimir Krzyanowski. Krzyanowski commanded troops from New York, but the U.S. Senate allegedly found it too difficult to pronounce his name and so would not confirm his promotion to general.

## Camp and Outpost Duty for Infantry

The provost duty of the Army of the Potomac as of February 1862 (will be responsible for) suppressing of marauding and depredations, and of all brawls and disturbances, preservation of good order and suppression of drunkenness beyond the limits of the camps as well as:

- Suppression of gambling houses, drinking houses or bar rooms, and brothels.
- Regulation of hotels, taverns, markets, and places of public amusement.
- Searches, seizures, and arrests.
- Execution of sentences of general courts-martial, involving imprisonment or capital punishment.
- Enforcement of orders prohibiting the sale of intoxicating liquors, whether by tradesmen or sutlers, and of orders respecting passes.

## Ambrose Burnside (1824–81), Union

Burnside took away fame from the war for something other than battle. While Doubleday was the general who did *not* invent baseball, Burnside was the general who invented a style of facial hair, originally called "burnsides," that we know today as "sideburns." At the time, having strips of hair extending down the cheek and connecting to the mustache, leaving the chin completely bare, was quite unusual.

At the First Battle of Bull Run, Burnside had superior forces but handed victory to the South when he did a poor job of managing that advantage. He was said to have fought defensively, parceling out troops to meet thrusts by the Confederates that served to negate his manpower advantage. As a result, Lincoln pulled Burnside out of direct troop leadership, essentially handing him a job away from the front after he lost several battles; he was successful after the war, both in business and as the governor of Rhode Island.

# Benjamin Franklin Butler (1818–93), Union

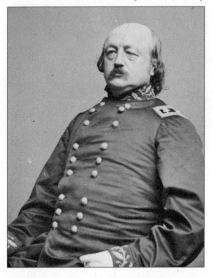

General Butler's claim to fame is one that most honorable soldiers would prefer not to have. In 1862, he was put in charge of New Orleans, whose capture early in the war provided a major advantage for the Union, shutting down a very important port.

Butler was involved in financial scandals while serving as military mayor in New Orleans. Once the war was over, he was successful doing something he desired far more than a military career—he was twice elected to Congress from the state of Massachusetts. While serving in Congress, Butler was a vigorous and vocal proponent of the impeachment of Andrew Johnson and was angered by the president's ability to withstand the impeachment and remain in office.

## Camp and Outpost Duty for Infantry

A daily evacuation of the bowels is indispensable to bodily health, vigor, and endurance.

## George Meade (1815–72), Union

General Meade, selected by Lincoln to become the commander of the Army of the Potomac just three days before the Battle of Gettysburg, was later relieved of his position, which had become a bit of a revolving door as Lincoln grew dissatisfied with the various generals, including Meade.

The general was wounded in two battles, severely in the Seven Days Battle (in the back, arm and side) and later in the hip at Antietam, but he continued to lead his men. At Gettysburg, he was integral to the North's victory in the complex and oft-dissected battle. It was Meade who stopped Lee on the second day, and then was responsible for repelling the infamous Pickett's Charge.

### Camp and Outpost Duty for Infantry

Soldiers must not be permitted to leave the ranks to strip or rob the dead, nor even to assist the wounded unless by express permission.

But Meade will be remembered for what transpired at Gettysburg after the Union victory. Many felt that he had an opportunity to end the war at that moment, at that place, but Meade let the retreating Lee go when he had a clear opportunity to pursue the withdrawing and depleted Confederate troops under Lee's command. Of course, today it is only conjecture, but many believe that the Southern forces were in such bad shape that they could have been defeated so soundly at that point that the war might have been over two years earlier than it was.

### Joshua Chamberlain (1828–1914), Union

Chamberlain was professor of languages at Bowdoin College in Maine when the war began and enlisted as a colonel in the 20th Maine Volunteer Infantry. He saw action in at least two dozen battles, each time leading troops in one capacity or another. He was wounded six times and lost his horse in battle several times, nearly losing his life at Gettysburg when his mount was shot out from under him.

General Grant assigned Chamberlain to receive the surrender at Appomattox, and Chamberlain, an intelligent and compassionate man, demonstrated why he was selected, having his troops show respect to the defeated Confederates by saluting all of them as they marched past.

## George McClellan (1826–85), Union

Unlike many generals who began inauspiciously at West Point, George McClellan was an engineer and graduated second in his class at the Military Academy. He went right from West Point to fight in the war with Mexico. He studied war both technically and strategically, eventually writing about military tactics.

McClellan was referred to as "Little Mac" by his troops, who were fiercely loyal to their commander. At one point, he led an army of more than 100,000 men as general of the Army of the Potomac.

For all his strengths, McClellan had glaring weaknesses as well, the major one being that he was too cautious and conservative, often overestimating the size of enemy forces in battle. At one point, Lee's army pushed into Maryland allegedly because he knew McClellan's position and his propensity to overstate the enemy strength; Lee thought he would be able to regain previously lost ground. The result was the Battle of Antietam, in which Lee was not as successful as he had assumed, and both sides suffered horrible losses. McClellan's apparent "refusal" to follow Lee as he retreated after the battle angered Lincoln, who then relieved the general of his command, replacing him with Ambrose Burnside.

McClellan had been a political antagonist and was clearly a man with ambition from the earliest days of the war. He outlined his own personal plans to attack the Confederates and mount assaults into the South before the war began; he was rebuffed by his commander, Winfield Scott, who was, at the time, the only man who outranked the young, energetic general. McClellan's political and military clout came from a close relationship with former Ohio governor and Lincoln's Secretary of the Treasury, Salmon Chase. McClellan was tasked with forming the Army of the Potomac, which he did with great speed and management skill. McClellan's small battle victories seemed to make him a national hero, and he wrote his wife at one point in this early stage of the war that "Presdt, Cabinet, Genl Scott & all deferring to me—by some strange operation of magic I seem to have become *the* power of the land..."

McClellan wrote to his wife after the Battle of Antietam, a tactical draw and the bloodiest battle in American history, but one that stopped Lee's invasion, turned the war in the North's favor and, of course, angered Lincoln because Lee's

## Camp and Outpost Duty for Infantry

Officers are never to give permission to any man to quit the ranks excepting an account of illness, or for some other absolutely necessary purpose.

army was allowed to retreat uncontested. He told her he felt his genius went unrecognized: "Those in whose judgment I rely tell me that I fought the battle splendidly and that it was a masterpiece of art....I feel I have done all that can be asked in twice saving the country....Well, one of these days history will I trust do me justice."

Lincoln and his cabinet were incensed at McClellan's continual overestimating of his Confederate counterpart's troop strength; McClellan often claimed the troops he faced had a two-to-one edge over his own, when, in fact, it was typically just the opposite.

McClellan became more offensive; instead of chasing the enemy, he chose to chase Lincoln, running against him as a democrat in the coming election. However, he was soundly defeated, as Lincoln was easily reelected for a second term.

## James Ewell Brown "Jeb" Stuart (1833–64), Confederate

Stuart graduated from the U.S. Military Academy at West Point just in time to be handed an ugly job—dealing with the chaos caused by abolitionist John Brown at Harpers Ferry. Although he was enlisted in the U.S. Army, when the war broke out, Stuart did not hesitate to resign his commission in favor of fighting for his home state of Virginia.

He was given a commission as a colonel in the 1st Virginia Cavalry. In the First Battle of Bull Run, it was Stuart's men who chased down the retreating Union forces to cause a surprising and humiliating defeat for the North at the beginning of what was supposed to be a quick, easy Union victory. The feat earned Stuart a promotion to brigadier general, and he was later made a major general. He became well known in both the North and the South for his tactics and skill in leading mounted troops.

One of many problems that the South faced in the war that the North did not was a constant drain of important manpower. Besides the loss of tens of thousands of enlisted men, the Confederate army lost far more leaders than the Union army, and it was devastating.

Gettysburg was a crushing defeat in many ways for the South, and, certainly, failing on the push into Union territory was huge. But a staggering number of officers were killed there, and Stonewall Jackson was fatally wounded just prior to the battle.

In the spring of 1864, Stuart was killed in battle with Sheridan's troops, which were marching toward Richmond. The two generals' forces engaged there, and Stuart was severely wounded and died the next day in a hospital in Richmond.

## Camp and Outpost Duty for Infantry

Keep the hair of the head closely cut, say within an inch and a half of the scalp in every part, repeated on the first of each month, and wash the whole scalp plentifully in cold water every morning.

# Robert E. Lee (1807–70), Confederate

Lee was perhaps the most popular and revered general throughout the South during the Civil War, and was certainly one of, if not the most respected among the ranks of enlisted men and officers on both sides of the conflict.

Lee was the son of Revolutionary War hero Harry (Henry) "Light Horse" Lee and graduated from West Point second in his class in 1829. During the Civil War, Lee suffered the typical situation that all his commanders faced—being outnumbered on the battlefield. He took his losses humbly and personally, and by the time he was finally forced to surrender (after two years of being beaten down), his troops were ridiculously outnumbered.

After the surrender, Lee was offered a position as president of Washington College in Virginia, where he improved both the college and the standard of education there. He also encouraged his former troops to consider an education. Lee believed that Southerners should think of themselves as Americans first, not Southerners or Virginians or Texans.

The college thrived, and Lee's life moved on—he was never interested in discussing the war or writing his memoirs about it. Unfortunately, his life was cut short when he suffered a stroke and died suddenly just five years after the end of the Civil War.

## Pierre Gustave Toutant (P.G.T.) Beauregard (1818–93), Confederate

With his very French Creole name, Louisiana-born Beauregard instantly became famous in the Civil War because he was the commander of the troops that started it! It is ironic that the tag that followed him around the rest of his life was as "the man who started the war," when, in fact, it was truly a "group" effort. The South, under Jefferson Davis, was very unified in the war effort.

Beauregard led Southern troops to victory in the First Battle of Bull Run. Later, while not losing the battle per se at Shiloh, Beauregard's forces suffered enormous losses. Battles such as Shiloh were like a heavyweight title fight. Although the conflict ended in a draw, the repeated punches to the South had a cumulative effect, far more than they did on the Northern forces. The Confederacy was already heavily outnumbered in men, supplies, weapons and ammunition, and every battle it won or lost had a negative effect on its army.

Both before and after the war, Beauregard was in demand for his engineering skills. While a student at West Point, he built a reputation for his prowess in artillery command and military engineering. In an odd twist, the Egyptian government offered him a position as the leader of its military; the general declined and remained with the Confederate army for the last year of the war. At the end of the conflict, he returned to his home in New Orleans, where he wrote *The Principles and Maxims of the Art of War*.

## Jubal Early (1816–94), Confederate

Early had a reputation as one of the meanest generals on either side during the Civil War. During the battle of Gettysburg, he led his men to York, Pennsylvania, where they occupied the city for a short period of time. It was the largest city occupied or taken by the Confederates during the entire war.

As a student at West Point, Early did well until he was expelled for fighting with another cadet, and the incident led to bad blood between the two throughout their service as Confederate officers during the war. Between the Mexican War and the Civil War, Early studied for and passed the bar; he was practicing law when the war broke out and immediately enlisted in the Confederate army.

Early was promoted to brigadier general after the First Battle of Bull Run in July 1861. In that battle, his valor impressed General P.G.T. Beauregard. He fought in most of the major battles in the eastern campaigns, including the Seven Days Battles, the Second Battle of Bull Run, Antietam, Fredericksburg, Chancellorsville, Gettysburg and numerous battles in the Shenandoah Valley.

Later in the war, he was relieved of his command by General Lee for insubordination, despite the fact that Lee was a great supporter of Early and considered him an outstanding soldier. Early lived in Mexico for a time after the war, fearing that the U.S. government would try him as a traitor for fighting against the Union, which never happened. He returned to Virginia in 1869, where he continued to practice law.

Early was also a devout white supremacist, but that was a vastly different label than in the 21st century. He believed simply that God made men different colors to distinguish

## Camp and Outpost Duty for Infantry

If your men stop in spite of your energetic exhortations and efforts, if they give way, do not endeavor to keep them near the enemy when their courage fails, and draw them back behind a shelter, or behind other troops, and when the danger has become less, and you hope that your authority and the voice of duty will be obeyed, rally them...

one race as being subordinate to the other. Early commented that since it would be impractical to transport the blacks back to Africa, they should remain in the U.S.: "The conditions of domestic slavery, as it existed in the South, had not only resulted in a great improvement in the moral and physical condition of the Negro race, but had furnished a class of laborers as happy and contented as any in the world," though perhaps just a few would disagree with him!

## Braxton Bragg (1817–76), Confederate

Bragg was a controversial Confederate general. One thing he did accomplish was a rare victory for the South at Chickamauga, but this was offset by his reluctance to engage in battle when ordered to do so and when circumstances certainly would have suggested it.

Bragg was overly fastidious in many other parts of his military service. He was organized and efficient, some said to a fault. When dire casualties limited the number of Confederate generals available, each was needed every minute at the front, but Bragg was serving in two capacities, the other being as post quartermaster, distributing supplies to his troops.

The consensus was that Bragg had a lot more to give but was never able to show himself at his organized, conscientious and disciplined best. In virtually every battle he entered, his Confederate troops were far outnumbered by the North. It was often all that Lee's generals could do to put their creative military skills to use to stave off defeat and hope to come away with a standoff—a psychological victory, at least.

## George Pickett (1825–75), Confederate

Pickett's name evokes virtually the same response regardless who you ask. It was Pickett whose ill-timed charge at the Battle of Gettysburg helped turn that conflict into a resounding Southern defeat.

It was there that the dapper Confederate saw his first major action of the war, and it was there that he led the famous (or infamous) charge directly into the heart of the Northern defenses. Brave and determined, Pickett's troops suffered enormous losses in the charge. He was embittered for the rest of the war, insisting he was only following Lee's orders, while the debate raged about whether he was indeed doing so or whether he took it upon himself to make the ill-fated attack in the hope of turning the tide with a victorious charge.

After the war, Pickett, like many Southerners who fought against the Union, feared reprisals or imprisonment for actions that might have been viewed as treason. Lincoln issued a general amnesty, and though more than a few in the South did not believe it immediately at the end of the war, they soon found out that they could return to their homes with no fear of being arrested.

## Camp and Outpost Duty for Infantry

On marches and in the field, the only mess furniture of the soldier will be one tin plate, one tin cup, one knife, fork, and spoon, to each man, to be carried by himself.

## William Quantrill (1837–65), Confederate

Quantrill led one of the nastiest pseudo-army groups in the Civil War. As "partisan rangers," essentially guerrilla fighters, they were given status as Confederate soldiers, and Quantrill, as leader, recruited his own men and gave them rank and status directly.

Unlike others who operated under the same basic structure, Quantrill had no scruples, and "Quantrill's Raiders" became notorious for sneak attacks not just on Union soldiers, but also on innocent citizens doing nothing but walking down a street. Quantrill followed the Kansas-Nebraska debates about slavery with an eye to ending the disputes by killing everyone he could find on the wrong side of the argument.

At one point, he and his men rode into Lawrence, Kansas, and methodically shot people walking along the city streets. He also led a group of raiders estimated at 800 strong when he first reached Kansas.

Union troops had been sent to Kansas to protect residents, but Quantrill's Raiders were not a small or ragtag group. They were systematic and very good at what they did and they had a full company of men, not just five or ten. The Raiders had two real missions: the first was to kill as many Kansans and abolitionists as possible, and the second was to rob everyone they killed to line their own pockets.

It took the U.S. government until 1865 to catch up to Quantrill, when his dwindling manpower (he was down to perhaps just a dozen men, the others dead or riding with someone else by then) finally removed whatever advantage he had. Using Quantrill's own tactics, the U.S. Army ambushed and killed him.

Some of his gang formed their own group after the war, but with no pretense toward either political or social goals. One such group included a number of thieves who formed the nucleus of the James-Younger Gang. They used the same tactics as Quantrill had during the war, relying on quick, daring attacks on horseback—to rob trains.

## Camp and Outpost Duty for Infantry

When the sentinel hears or discovers any thing suspicious in the direction of the enemy, as, for instance, the moving of trains or troops, camp-fires, smoke, rising of dust or glittering of arms, cutting timber, driving nails, etc., he should signal to the corporal of the outposts, who, in turn, will signal to the officer of the pickets.

Much like other Confederate and Union veterans' organizations that met annually in states and nationally, veterans who had served under Quantrill did the same in the years after the war.

## Thomas "Stonewall" Jackson (1824–63), Confederate

Jackson was and still is regarded as one of the finest generals on either side during the Civil War. Having picked up his education piecemeal after both his parents died, he still managed to gain admittance to the Military Academy at West Point. A dogged student, he was determined not to finish at the bottom of his class. He graduated after three years, by which time he had climbed to 17th in the graduating class. Other cadets commented that had Jackson remained for a fourth year, he surely would have moved all the way to the top of the next year's class.

Jackson was recognized for both intelligence and bravery in the Mexican-American War, and between that conflict and the Civil War, he was ordered to provide military support for the hanging of abolitionist John Brown following the latter's armed slave revolt at Harpers Ferry, Virginia.

In 1851, Jackson accepted a teaching post at the Virginia Military Institute, where his material on military strategy and technique remained part of the curriculum for years because of its basic application and logic in battle. He was also recognized as a tough taskmaster while drilling recruits.

In the Confederate army, Jackson proved his value repeatedly. It was at the First Battle of Bull Run that Jackson earned his nickname "Stonewall" for being just that against the Union troops.

There are no estimates or detailed information on the number of Civil War deaths from friendly fire, but it can be assumed, based the huge numbers of soldiers engaged in small areas and the often inconsistent weapons (and the inexperience of many of those using them) that thousands could have been killed accidentally by their own troops.

On May 2, 1863, Jackson and his party were returning to camp at Chancellorsville and were fired upon twice when their response to challenges by pickets were assumed to be a trick by a Union company. Several men were killed in the chaos, and Jackson was wounded twice in the left arm and once in the right hand. Doctors amputated the arm, and he was cared for in a house near the battlefield. The general died eight days later from pneumonia while recovering from the wounds and surgery. He was just 39 years old, and on many occasions, Lee and others commented that the loss of Jackson was a major turning point in the war.

## Camp and Outpost Duty for Infantry

No refuse, slops, or excrement should be allowed to be deposited in the trenches for drainage around the tents.

# John S. Mosby (1833–1916), Confederate

Mosby, known as the "Gray Ghost" for his elusiveness, out-lived a great many Southern officers. He spent only a brief time in military service, instead serving as a commander for a group of partisan rangers—a group that could play by its own rules and did not have to follow the normal conventions of war. The rangers were scouts, spies and guerrillas, generally maneuvering behind enemy lines.

Mosby often walked unnoticed among the enemy in Washington, DC, and at one point, he captured a Union general, having befriended him at a bar and then stealthily taken him away once he was drunk.

Partisan rangers like Mosby created such havoc that many Northern officers took to executing them if captured. At one point, Custer did this to a group of Mosby's men, so Mosby in turn captured a group of Custer's men and executed them, sending the bodies back to Custer, one of which had a note on it stating that he would cease the arbitrary executions if the Union did likewise—and they did.

Mosby was captured during the war and imprisoned, but he was somehow released and went right back into action. He was arrested immediately after the end of the war, but then let go. He went back to his law practice, which he continued for many years. He passed away in 1916 at the age of 82.

During the Civil War, partisan rangers were all viewed the same way—as uncontrolled and uncontrollable guerilla soldiers. But when examining such men individually, it becomes obvious that their motives and actions were very different, for example, Mosby versus Quantrill.

## James Longstreet (1821–1904), Confederate

Known as "Old War Horse," Longstreet was one of the most successful Confederate generals. He openly disagreed with Lee over offensive plans at the Battle of Gettysburg (and was proven correct). There were too many errors made in tactical warfare and planning in that pivotal battle, and the South lost more than just a horrendous number of men—it lost a great deal of ground in the war and ultimately sealed its own defeat, even though it took nearly two more years to end the conflict.

Longstreet, fiercely loyal to the Confederate cause, later found post-war jobs in government. He held appointive offices under presidents Grant, Roosevelt and McKinley.

## Camp and Outpost Duty for Infantry

The officer of the guard will see that the company cooks are called in time in the morning to prepare the coffee and breakfast for the men before Reveille.

# ON THE HOME FRONT

Civil War newspapers

❧

## All the News

As long as the conflict continued, the Civil War *was* the United States. The war was all consuming and, as has so often been said, pitted brother against brother. Every newspaper had reports of the battles, not just an article on page one and another somewhere at the back of the paper, but entire front pages and much of the inside of typically eight-to-twelve-page newspapers were devoted to reports on every aspect of the war. It consumed the economy, daily activities and the life of every family. Fathers, brothers, husbands, uncles, sons, nephews—often two or three or more from each family—were involved in the war and often fought against one another.

# The Prison Show

An article appeared under "Amusements" in the *Philadelphia Press* on December 12, 1865, describing a presentation that the Philadelphia Academy of Music was preparing that would show what conditions were like at the horrible Southern prison, Andersonville. Former Union soldiers were employed for the event to create scenery and provide details of what transpired there. If the presentation was a success, the producers planned to take the show on the road to the "Eastern, Southern and Western States." There was no report on how they would demonstrate scurvy, starvation and the 100 daily deaths in the camp, which was described by inmates as a living hell for those who managed to stay alive.

## "The Coming Celebration—The Field of Gettysburg"

The headline above is from the Providence, Rhode Island, *Bulletin* of October 27, 1863, announcing the nearly completed plans for the dedication of the cemetery that "contains seven acres, and includes the most remarkable part of the battle ground south of Gettysburg."

The article continued: "Edward Everett will deliver, probably, his finest oration, and an elegiac hymn, by Longfellow, will be sung by a combined force of the musical societies."

There was no mention of "a few appropriate remarks" by the president. His speech was announced shortly before the actual ceremony.

## Easing the Worries Back Home

Musicals and stage plays remained a big part of city life during the war, while in the rural areas, there were church socials and square dances when people could spare time away from their farms. But what could be better than a circus?

The touring Barnum American Museum offered a respite in the North's large cities during the war. What would America see? How about "A Hottentot, a Bushman, a Kaffir, a Zooloo, Aztec children, thirty monster snakes, African Savages and Miss Dora Dawron, the Double-Voiced Singer." Admission was just a quarter for adults and 15 cents for children. A wonderful way to forget the horrors of war, certainly, and replace them with the horrors of Barnum.

## Walt Whitman

Whitman certainly is one of the best-known American poets. *Leaves of Grass*, perhaps his greatest collection, was self-published six years before the start of the war because no publisher was interested, but by the time the Civil War started, he was beginning to attract a following. Although he wrote during the war about the battles and the men who fought them, he also worked for three years as a hospital aide, caring for recuperating soldiers in the North. His poem "O Captain, My Captain" was written about Lincoln after the president was assassinated.

# Writing About the War

*Life Struggles in Rebel Prisons*, written by Captain Joseph Ferguson of the 1st New Jersey Volunteers, chronicled the stories of 20 different Confederate prisons. Published by the author, the 230-page book was $1.00 postpaid in December 1865. It was just one of a rash of books about the war that appeared throughout the U.S. in the months after the end of the conflict.

## Civil War Tokens—A Smart Move in Private Northern Coinage

While the South wallowed in horrible inflation and printed stacks of worthless currency, the North didn't have an inflation issue, though it did have a precious metal shortage.

The U.S. government couldn't strike an adequate number of one-cent pieces (pennies) for general use because most of the country's copper and bronze had been diverted to the war effort. People began hoarding the large-size cent coins from before the war, as well as the new Flying Eagle and Indian Head pennies that followed, as their value in copper exceeded their face value. To combat the shortage of federally struck coins, private merchants began creating their own tokens to substitute for pennies.

The tokens were minted in two types: "patriotics," which carried a patriotic message supporting the Union but were generally without advertisements; and "store cards," which advertised businesses from restaurants and saloons to black-smiths and bookstores. They sometimes also carried a patriotic message or a bust of Washington, Franklin or Lincoln.

The tokens allowed businesses to advertise, and they were handed out instead of pennies for change on purchases. The tokens cost less than a cent to make, so they were a profitable sideline for merchants. During the course of the war, before private coinage was made illegal in 1864, an astounding 50 million one-cent tokens were made in an estimated 10,000 different designs and varieties. Today, as collectors' items, they are worth anywhere up to hundreds of dollars, depending on a token's rarity and condition.

## In God We Trust

The 1864 law that made it illegal to produce tokens and use them in commerce also added the phrase to our coins that has remained ever since: In God We Trust.

The phrase was used for the first time on the unusual and short-lived U.S. two-cent piece.

## Edward Everett

One of the foremost orators of the Civil War era, Edward Everett was exceptionally knowledgeable about national politics. In the election of 1860, he was actually the vice presidential candidate of something called the Constitutional Union Party, which supported the Constitution and refused to take sides between the North and South immediately before the war. He ran with presidential candidate and wealthy slave owner John Bell, but garnered just three percent of the vote.

It was Everett only three years later who was called on to deliver the keynote address at the dedication of the Gettysburg cemetery. He spoke for two hours, followed by "a few appropriate remarks" by President Lincoln. While the press both lauded and criticized Lincoln's comments, Everett said he wished he could have come "as near the central idea of the occasion" in two hours as Lincoln did in two minutes.

# BLACK SOLDIERS SHOWED THEIR BRAVERY

*During the Civil War and the last 150 years or so since, virtually everyone would answer the question the same way: What was the war about? Slavery! But the real issue was states' rights and whether or not a state could override the federal government and choose to be a slave state. But for millions of black men and women, the war was about freedom—freedom from slavery and the right for free men to fight for the freedom of their brothers and sisters still in the bonds of slavery in the South.*

A broadside for the enlistment of black soldiers

Company E, 4th U.S. Colored Infantry at Fort Lincoln, Maryland

## Hungry to Prove Their Worth

It took a long time for the United States to grant combat positions to black soldiers—allowing them to die heroes, but to die nevertheless. Most people were, and are, unaware that throughout the course of the Civil War, nine percent of the total Union army consisted of black soldiers. Even in the supposedly less racist North, there were fears that black soldiers would panic in the face of battle, in the face of Southern rifles. There was also concern that they were not smart enough to understand how to march and load their guns and shoot—that they were simply stupid compared to Northern white soldiers.

There was also concern that black troops would be murdered by Confederate soldiers, and with good reason—the Confederate government announced they would not take black prisoners, and would shoot them on the spot instead.

Even though black men in uniform were held out of combat until late in the war, there was still plenty of opportunity to die. Roughly one-third died as a result of being in the military. Disease and sickness were responsible for some 30 times more black deaths than combat!

## The Fort Pillow Massacre

Fort Pillow, Tennessee, became a horrible footnote in U.S. history and a painful but high point in the struggle for recognition of the nation's black soldiers. When the fort was overrun by the Confederates and they saw they had been fighting black troops, they became incensed and indiscriminately murdered both black and white soldiers who had surrendered.

White officers and black soldiers in a colored regiment

## Black Soldiers Fought on Both Sides in the War

Few studying the Civil War in depth for the first time are surprised by the fact that black Americans fought heroically in the war, because the story of the 54th Massachusetts has been told in many ways. So have other stories of the bravery of Union soldiers and sailors. But about the black Americans fighting for the Confederacy? Estimates are that as many as 60,000 to 65,000 black soldiers were in the Confederate army during the war, and that 20 percent of those actually saw combat. Initially, the Confederate Congress only approved of non-combat roles for blacks, but even with that mandate in place, Southern commanders and militia officers welcomed black men into their units if they passed a simple, one-question test: "Will you fight?"

Jefferson Davis was reputed to have outlined plans for a Colored Confederate army, with paid bounties for enlisting. Had the plan come to fruition, it might have thrown the entire Southern slavery structure into chaos. But the war ended before any such scheme could be developed and slavery—and the Confederacy—came to an end in 1865.

## Camp and Outpost Duty for Infantry

A soldier will be more likely to respect himself when he sees that his officer respects him.

# A Not-So-Small(s) Hero

One very large name in the black struggle during the Civil War was Robert Smalls, a Southern slave who proved himself a hero in many ways. He orchestrated one of the most daring escapes by a group of slaves, and he did so by stealing a recently overhauled $30,000 gunboat.

Smalls worked, hired out for his master, at the Charleston shipyard from the age of 12, and thus was not just comfortable with but very knowledgeable about vessels and the waterfront.

He was 23 years old when the war began. At the time, he was working with eight other slaves crewing on the *Planter*, a sidewheeler refitted as a Confederate gunboat. A veteran of 11 years on the Charleston waterfront even though he was just 23 years old, Smalls had worked as a pilot, assisting large vessels in and out of the harbor, and now was crewing on the newly outfitted gunboat along with other slaves. Smalls hatched a bold plan to steal the *Planter* and told his family and the other slaves with whom he worked that they were leaving the following morning, taking family members with them.

The risk was a simple matter of life and death; if they were caught stealing a Confederate ship and escaping from their owners, they would be shot, without question. It was life and death for the slaves' families, as well, whom the crewmembers planned to smuggle to the shipyard during the night.

Smalls and his crew were supposed to be on the ship at night, so Confederate guards thought nothing of them apparently working on the gunboat, and they ignored women and children who came to the ship as well. It was common for other slaves to bring food to the crew at night. Early in the morning, before the white officers came on board, Smalls fired up the boiler and slowly eased the ship out of its moorage. Without incident, the ship sailed slowly into the harbor, flying the Confederate flag. If someone saw it, they no doubt thought the crew was merely testing the ship's engine, and no one could see the slaves below decks.

## Camp and Outpost Duty for Infantry

Ammunition issued will be inspected frequently. Each man will be made to pay for the rounds expended without orders, or not in the way of duty, or which may be damaged or lost by his neglect.

Smalls sailed the ship into open water and lowered the Confederate flag, raising the white flag instead. He took the ship north and delivered the refurbished gunboat to the Union navy.

His reward was a commission in the Colored Naval Corps, and he later replaced the captain of the *Planter* after saving the ship and crew during a heavy battle with a Confederate gunboat. Smalls was invaluable as a sailor and captain, and the small, heavily gunned ship was a welcome addition to the sparse Union navy.

## Camp and Outpost Duty for Infantry

Messes will be prepared by privates of squads, including private musicians, each taking his tour. The greatest care should be observed in washing and scouring the cooking utensils.

# HOW DOES ONE JUDGE A PERSON TO BE FREE?

## Freedom of the Press

William Lloyd Garrison was one of the most influential voices against slavery in the United States and publisher of *The Liberator* newspaper, which was often quoted and had its articles reprinted throughout both the North and the South before and during the war. Garrison started *The Liberator* in 1831, the year of the bloody Nat Turner slave revolt, and continued publishing during and after the war. Like many others, Garrison provided a voice for emancipation, freedom and rights for black Americans (and Confederates!), which was instrumental in the fight for freedom that lasted much longer than the Civil War.

"Contrabands"

## Human Contraband

While most people are familiar with the meaning of the term "contraband," which is typically defined as goods that have been imported or exported illegally, you'll need to check a Civil War dictionary for the most creative use of the word. The architect of the Civil War definition of the term and its application was General Benjamin Butler, who was an attorney prior to the war.

When three slaves who were contracted to the Confederate army by their owners as a work party escaped near Hampton Roads (of *Monitor* and *Merrimac* fame), they rowed a boat to the Union lines in southeast Virginia and asked for asylum (freedom) from the Northern soldiers.

Prior to the war, U.S. law required the return of "fugitive slaves" to their owners. Butler, however, when asked by a Confederate officer for the return of the slaves as required by law, replied that Virginia was not part of the Union but was instead a foreign power at war with the United States. As such, Butler said that he would retain the slaves as "contraband of war."

Word of that decision traveled incredibly fast and slaves, not just one or two or a dozen, but hundreds, began escaping and requesting that they be declared "contrabands" and given their freedom. Although there were no laws that granted them freedom, they set up camps near Union troops and worked for minimal pay for the army. Former slave women earned equally small wages as cooks and washerwomen. In their eyes, they were free—no owner, no overseer, no whippings, no fear, just a new life as the war continued. Another law was passed that did not declare the slaves free, but made them legal contraband of war and allowed them to stay where they settled near Union troops.

Abolitionists, teachers and clergy in the North assisted the contrabands and taught them to read, among other things, which was illegal in the South.

The former slaves reveled in the Emancipation Proclamation, issued in September 1862, which many could read by the time Lincoln delivered it. Freedom finally came in the complete legal sense in late 1865, after the war and after Lincoln was dead, with the Congressional ratification of the 13th Amendment, which abolished slavery in the United States.

## Camp and Outpost Duty for Infantry

The field officer of the day will visit each line, after supervising the posting, at least once during the day and twice during the night.

# WHEN IT WASN'T THE WAR, IT WAS THE POLITICS

## Little Tangible Change, But a Huge Impression

The Emancipation Proclamation has been evaluated and criticized for a century and a half as the law that freed slaves who were already free—and did nothing for those who weren't.

In legal terms, the proclamation preserved the neutrality of the Border States, but did little else. It freed the slaves in the Confederate states, where Lincoln had no authority, of course. The value of the proclamation was not just that it incensed slave owners, but that it sent a message to slaves throughout the South. It freed the slaves in the North where Lincoln had authority, but, of course, there were no slaves in the North. And it did nothing in the Border States, which pleased them and kept them part of the United States, which Lincoln desperately wanted to do. That in itself was no small task and of vital necessity for the North during the early stages of the war.

## When Slavery Goes, So Go the Slaves?

In the North, opinions about slavery and what would happen when it was abolished were plentiful in spite of, or perhaps because of, the war. One view was that once slavery had been eliminated throughout the country, assuming that the United States were once again united, all the former slaves should be deported! No one believed that they should be returned to whatever country in Africa from which they had been captured, but suggestions were that they would "naturally" relocate to "the West Indies, Central America and South America." Stronger voices in the North suggested perhaps that the South should keep the "proven Negro workers and deport the white drunkards and bar-room loungers." There was no paucity of suggestions during the war, just an excess of "experts"!

Harriet Beecher Stowe

## *Uncle Tom's Cabin* Began in an Abolitionist Magazine

Abolitionist Harriet Beecher Stowe would have to be given credit for the most influential book of the Civil War era, but it seems a bit of a stretch to say that it was the cause of the war, as some have claimed. Stowe wrote the book as a serialization in *The National Era*, an abolitionist paper, and as a result of its success, agreed to turn it into a book. That was in 1852, nine years before the Confederate States of American attacked Fort Sumter.

It is difficult to confirm publishing statistics for the era, but the book was said to be the number-two seller the following year with 300,000 copies—second only to the Bible. It sold millions of copies in the 19th century in the U.S. and abroad, and comparable numbers since.

Stowe wrote her novel to make America—and the rest of the world—aware of the suffering of slaves. She viewed her characters as steadfast Christians who never turned to hate despite ultimately being whipped to death. But along the way, modern readers and society picked up stereotypes and epithets from the book: Uncle Tom became the acquiescent black man, not the hero, while such affectionate terms as "mammy" and "pickaninny" likewise "turned South" in the minds of Americans. One character, the cruel overseer, Simon Legree, has remained in our vernacular as the definition of an evil, heartless man.

## A Key to the Book, *the* Key to the Book

*A Key to Uncle Tom's Cabin*, a little-known book by Stowe, followed the controversy and massive sales of *Uncle Tom's Cabin* a year after the first book was published. She wrote the 1853 guide to explain her characters and the purpose and story of her book, since the original was met with substantial criticism, though the positive response was overwhelming.

### Camp and Outpost Duty for Infantry

It is seldom expedient to send verbal reports; it should be avoided if possible, as it is very difficult to find non-commissioned officers or soldiers capable of delivering them correctly.

## In the Era of the Iron Horse, She was the Conductor

During the Civil War, the railroads played a major part in the success of the North and, briefly, in early successes of the South. They were vital for troop and munitions movements for both sides, and it was big news when the U.S. cut lines, ripped up tracks and destroyed vital rail links in the South.

One of the most important railroads ran from the Deep South to the North—the Underground Railroad, the freedom train for which Harriet Tubman was known as the conductor.

A slave herself, Tubman had once suffered a fractured skull as a teenager when she tried to save another slave from a beating. That beating, one of many she suffered as a child, left her physically impaired, suffering headaches and seizures for the rest of her long life.

Tubman escaped slavery and made her way to freedom and the North in 1849. Often such escapes "to the North… from the South" were as much a political as a geographical statement. The miles may not have been long, but they were arduous and dangerous. Tubman's escape was from Maryland to Philadelphia, not a great distance in today's terms.

The Underground Railroad had no steel tracks, powerful engines or wooden cars. Rather, it was a network of secret routes with "stations" along the way where passengers could be hidden, obtain food and water and continue on their journey toward freedom.

Tubman, besides being known as the conductor on this special railroad and helping countless slaves escape to the North, was also known as "Moses" because she took so many to the Promised Land. Tubman enjoyed saying that she "never lost a passenger!" She traveled back and forth often; after her 1849 escape, she returned South repeatedly to free members of her family.

Tubman also posed as an old plantation slave woman when in the South, spying on Confederate activity for the Union army. She was so despised for what she did for slaves that during the war, there was a $40,000 bounty offered for her capture. (In comparison, there was a $100,000 price tag on John Wilkes Booth after Lincoln's assassination.)

Tubman worked another half century of her life helping secure rights for black Americans after the Civil War. She was unsure of her exact year of birth, 1820 or 1821, making her about 93 when she passed away in 1913, a resident of the home for elderly black former slaves that she helped found decades earlier.

---

**September 22, 1862**

Lincoln issues the Emancipation Proclamation.

---

## Sojourner Truth

An inspiring abolitionist, Sojourner Truth brought crowds to their feet when she spoke. It helped that she was six feet tall, an unusual sight in the middle of the 19th century, and she worked tirelessly to free slaves during the Civil War.

Truth had been a slave herself, but escaped *almost 40 years* before the war began. Interestingly, she lived in New York—as a slave—before slavery was made illegal in that state, but escaped to freedom prior to it being outlawed there.

Truth was a vibrant speaker, and she vowed to devote her life to the cause once she escaped. She used money she raised at speaking engagements to purchase a variety of basic necessities to distribute to black Union troops.

## Mary Elizabeth Bowser

A black slave in Virginia, Bowser was freed as a young woman. She worked in Richmond, Virginia, for Elizabeth Van Lew, an undercover supporter of the Union. Van Lew approached Bowser and asked her if she would work as a spy. When Bowser agreed, Van Lew sent her to work as an on-loan house slave—for Confederate president Jefferson Davis. No one in the household even considered that she might be able to read; it was illegal to teach slaves to read and write in the South.

Bowser listened carefully to conversations at dinner when guests dined with Davis, and she read every note or document left around the residence. Then she passed on the information to Van Lew, who sent it directly to Union military leaders.

# Roger B. Taney

Chief Justice of the U.S. Supreme Court, Roger B. Taney was an abomination in the judiciary system of the country. He single-handedly slowed improvements in the treatment of slaves and the eventual abolition of slavery. He also butchered the ideals of the Constitution and the role of the Supreme Court.

The landmark Dred Scott case in 1857 examined the question that if a slave is taken by his master into a free state, does the slave become free or have the right to sue for freedom because slavery is illegal in that state?

Taney did not just rule against Dred Scott, he proceeded to hand down rulings and opinions that were not part of the proceedings and to force his views about slavery onto the court, the country and Dred Scott. Scott thus remained a slave and was told unequivocally by Taney that he was not a man and thus was not entitled to sue. The judge added that the framers of the Constitution had made no specifications for slaves because they specifically were *not* people but property.

The Dred Scott case obviously inflamed the race and slavery issue even more; it was just four years until the Civil War would start.

Articulate former slave and abolitionist Frederick Douglass took—or at least said he took—a positive approach to all the negative judicial precedents created by Taney. Now, he said, at least the issue would be in front of the American people.

## From Taney's Decision in the Dred Scott Case

"The Question is simply this: Can a Negro, whose ancestors were imported into this country and sold as slaves, become a member of the political community formed and brought into existence by the Constitution of the United States, and as such become entitled to all the rights, and privileges, and immunities guaranteed by that instrument to the citizen? One of which rights is the privilege of suing in a court of the United States in the cases specified in the Constitution..."

Further, Taney said: "To all this mass of proof we have still to add, that Congress has repeatedly legislated upon the same construction of the Constitution that we have given...

The first of these acts is the naturalization law [of] Mar 26, 1790 [that] confines the right of becoming citizens to 'aliens being free white persons'..."

Dred Scott was given his freedom by his owner on May 26, 1857, three months after his court case was rejected. He died at 59 years of age just 17 months later.

# DIFFERENT ROLES BUT IMPORTANT JOBS

*Women played many different roles in the Civil War, many that would be considered typical and logical, and many more that would surprise us today and would have shocked both men and women at the time. Without the nurses and without the Sanitary Commission and Sanitary Fairs, soldiers and the war effort would have struggled terribly. Female abolitionists were as vital as male ones, and many who will remain forever unknown were spies or combat soldiers and were also critical to the Union. In smaller numbers, but so important, were the doctors on the battlefield and behind the lines.*

## Managing 3000 Nurses Under Hellish Conditions

Long before she was in charge of the entire Union nurses corps, Dorothea Dix was a veteran of other wars—wars on behalf of those who could not care for themselves and wars against state and federal politicians.

Dix was a pioneer in the care of the "indigent insane and the deaf, dumb and blind," in the language of her era. She took her battle from state to state, conducting research in North Carolina, Massachusetts, Illinois and other states, and crisscrossing America to show state legislators the abhorrent conditions in which indigent handicapped Americans lived and suffered. State after state established agencies for the care of these people, and her work eventually led to a federal bill being passed by both houses of Congress that set aside land on which to build hospitals and other care facilities.

But in 1854, President Franklin Pierce vetoed the bill, saying that it was not the federal government's job to commit itself

## Camp and Outpost Duty for Infantry

In hot climates the reveille will not be beaten until after sunrise; and hot coffee will be issued to the troops immediately after reveille roll call, as a preventive to the effects of malaria.

to social welfare, rather, it was the responsibility of the individual states. It was just one more example of the simmering battle of federal versus states' rights issues that was building toward war.

When the war finally started, Dix offered her services and was appointed Superintendent of Union Army Nurses. Although reports conflicted about the total number of female nurses working with Union doctors, most cited 3000 women under Dix's watch. One of her first actions was to hire only "middle-aged [over 30 years old] and plain-looking women," to ensure that she had serious nurses and not just young women looking to find husbands.

Dix required her nurses to dress alike in very plain, long skirts and to project a caring, maternal appearance. Her nurses, like the doctors, were faced with awful conditions, horrific wounds, high mortality rates and poor working conditions.

Union doctors and nurses were also asked to care for thousands of captured, wounded Confederate troops and did so with the same care that all the Northern wounded were afforded. This was, in many cases, difficult for nurses whose husbands were in battle, possibly wounded or killed while fighting the Confederates, but whether the casualties were from the South or the North, the soldiers were all effusive in their thanks for the care they received.

At Gettysburg alone, General Lee was forced to leave not only the dead on the battlefield, but 5000 wounded Confederate troops as well. There were often public outcries against

Union doctors and nurses caring for the enemy wounded, but Dix saw to it that all were treated and treated well. How would the Northern citizens, doctors and nurses feel if the Confederates refused to provide aid to injured Union troops?

Dix was tough, argumentative and persistent, which did not endear her to those in power. Her battles with military officers and government leaders ended before the war was over when she was relieved of her command of the nursing corps. She went back to tending those who had no one to champion their cause—the indigent, the disabled and the mentally ill—and to ensure that they were provided the most basic living conditions and care. She never stopped fighting for social reform and providing care for others, whether the wounded and misfortunate were soldiers, the mentally ill, the indigent or the disabled.

## Camp and Outpost Duty for Infantry

In case of being compelled to fire, the men on the right and left will go in (with) the one in the centre, and the three retire together—one should not retire without the other. If their pieces are discharged, they will retire upon the outposts in skirmishing order, with bayonets fixed.

## Angel of the Battlefield

Clara Barton, better known than Dorothea Dix, is often confused with Dix among those studying the war and the nursing corps. Barton, who also battled for civil rights, spent the war not just tending to battlefield wounded (riding in ambulances with frontline injured soldiers on the way back to the first line of medical care), but also formed the American Red Cross. She was known as the "Angel of the Battlefield" for seemingly appearing out of nowhere in the midst of battles to help care for and comfort the wounded.

Barton created the Red Cross and built it into an organization that would care for both military and private citizens in various disaster situations, not just war. It was intended to give aid in peacetime as well. Barton was responsible for seeing that supplies and lifesaving equipment and necessities were organized and then transported to frontline troops.

Even more importantly, she personally took on the daunting task of trying to locate and identify missing Union soldiers on the battlefields, in both the North and South. The number of missing and unidentified remains was unbelievably large. Beginning during the war and working until 1867, Barton personally located, researched and identified the remains of more than 20,000 soldiers. She was reported to have personally responded to more than 60,000 letters of inquiry about men missing in action.

Barton worked not just tirelessly, but endlessly on her self-appointed task of locating missing Union soldiers. She interviewed families, friends and soldiers in the same units, piecing together the battlefield history of men who never came home. So many battle site cemeteries throughout the country are scattered with grave markers that read simply "Five Unidentified Union Soldiers," "Four Unidentified Confederate Soldiers," "Eight Unidentified Union Soldiers" and so on. Her goal was more than just admirable; she wanted to be able to end the grief for families who did not know if their men were dead or possibly alive.

## Camp and Outpost Duty for Infantry

The contents of each and every wagon in the train should be known to all officers in charge or connected therewith.

With the help of Dorence Atwater, a young Union soldier, Barton was able to identify and lay to rest the remains of some 13,000 dead at the notorious Andersonville Confederate Prison. Unbeknownst to the Confederates, Atwater, a Union prisoner at Andersonville, was somehow able to obtain a list of those who had died there. After his release, he was determined to find a way to publish the list. He met Barton, and through her contacts, she assembled a group to go to the prison at the war's end. Barton, Atwater and 42 headstone carvers went to Andersonville to care for the remains of the dead Union soldiers, to identify as many bodies as possible and to bury them properly and mark the graves.

# Although
Clara Barton was known for identifying the remains of missing soldiers, after the war, the most intriguing "missing" item became her own headquarters office on 7th Street in Washington, DC. It's not known what year she gave up her small attic residence and office, but presumably in 1867. Some years later, the attic was boarded up, and over the years, it was forgotten, though the lower floors of the building saw more than a century of use. The building was slated for demolition in 1996, and someone happened to pull some boards loose, discovering that what was thought to be an unused crawl space or storage space was actually Clara Barton's former residence and office. Abandoned more than a century earlier, some of her papers and documents still remained in the space. The demolition was halted, and museum and government people came in to study and preserve the residence and its contents.

## Camp and Outpost Duty for Infantry

The kitchen should always be under the particular charge of a non-commissioned officer.

# CARING FOR THE WOUNDED WAS A WAR IN ITSELF

## Inside a Hastily Established Hospital in a Former Residence

"Out doors I notice a heap of amputated feet, legs, arms, hands, etc. a full load for a one-horse cart. Towards the river, are fresh graves, mostly of officers, their names on pieces of barrel-staves or broken boards, no system, but I have no doubt the best that can be done; all the wounds pretty bad, some frightful, unclean and bloody. Some of the wounded are rebel soldiers and officers, prisoners. One, a Mississippian, a captain, hit badly in leg, I talk'd with some time; he ask'd me for papers, which I gave him. (I saw him three months afterward in Washington, with his leg amputated, doing well.) I went through the rooms, downstairs and up. Some of the men were dying. I had nothing to give at that visit, but wrote a few letters to folks home."

–Notes written by poet Walt Whitman

## No Frankenstein, This

An important volume during the Civil War was *The Practice of Surgery* by Samuel Cooper, which provided detailed guides to bullet extraction, amputation and myriad other surgical practices. Most of the Civil War surgeons had never experienced battle conditions, and while they quickly became experts, this was their handbook along the way.

Union field hospital at Savage Station, Virginia

## Fifteen Minutes with Saw, File and Needle

Doctors on Civil War battlefields were taught to decide a soldier's fate quickly—the less-seriously injured and the mortally wounded were passed over so that physicians could save as many of the others as possible. In more cases than could be counted each day in a field hospital, that meant work with a special medical kit. Doctors had a surgical kit, a regular medical bag—and an amputation kit that contained canvas tourniquet belting, an amputation saw, scalpels and assorted other instruments for what became a highly efficient, if not a mechanized, operation.

Hands, arms, legs and feet were removed with skill and speed, both essential to save lives of patients. Doctors hoped that shock could be avoided if the operation was quick. Contrary to what many people have thought, there was no wholesale desire to amputate, but rather a necessity to save lives. Limbs hit with the typical, very heavy Civil War minié balls suffered dramatic injuries, and it was because of the ammunition, not lack of skill on the doctors' part, that limbs were amputated so incredibly often. Minié balls traveled slowly compared to modern bullets and were heavy and soft, meaning that when they made contact, they splayed out, and the soft but heavy lead balls smashed whatever was in their path—tissue, muscle, ligaments and bone.

The universal goal of the medics was to get the job done in an average of 15 minutes; some surgeons were so experienced that they could perform amputation surgery in only ten. Those were exceptions, however, as even 15 minutes was very fast, and each step required precise work.

Beginning the process of what would likely be an amputation, the surgeon first looked for an exit wound. If there was none, he felt inward from the open wound with a surgical probe, or more often his finger, to locate the bullet.

An assistant, or possibly a nurse, gave the patient a drink of whiskey to calm his nerves, then he was given chloroform (contrary to some rumors, both then and now, chloroform was available and soldiers did not have to "bite the bullet" while their limbs were amputated). If the soldier's limb needed to be removed, the surgeon first cut a large flap of skin—whether he was operating on an arm, leg or foot or hand—and laid it back above the incision he was making for the amputation. Next, he used a scalpel to cut away muscle and tissue, tied off arteries with thread, and then sawed through the bone. Finally, he used a file to smooth the end of the remaining bone, covered the stump with the flap he had cut and sewed the wound shut.

Fifteen minutes and on to the next patient.

## The Most Common Amputation

For all those amputated legs and arms, the most common amputation during the Civil War was that of one or more fingers. Fingers were subject to all sorts of abuse—broken skin, blisters, cuts, scrapes, bullet wounds (though to a lesser degree), and thus they constantly became infected, the major reason for amputation.

# PICK YOUR POISON— LITERALLY

## Another Civil War Enemy: Deadly Pyemia

One of the toughest battles in the Civil War was the fight against pyemia, a form of blood poisoning that occurred when bacteria-laden pus entered the bloodstream. Union doctors reported a 90 percent mortality rate if a patient contracted pyemia after surgery. It could come from any number of sources because of a general lack of cleanliness. Certainly, pyemia could have already been present in a wound, and surgical conditions were anything but sterile. If a doctor dropped an instrument during surgery, the best (and only!) option available to clean it was to rinse it in a pan of water—cold water that was likely already contaminated from other instruments used in the current surgery or the previous one.

Surgeons knew they had to be fast to avoid the possibility of shock, but they also wanted wounds open as briefly as possible. Doctors worked for hours in blood-and-tissue-spattered clothing. They had no antiseptic to wash hands or instruments, and would rinse both in the same pan of water they were forced to use for much of their work without rest, fresh water or antiseptics. Working slower would only have increased the mortality rate.

### Camp and Outpost Duty for Infantry

Haversacks will be marked upon the flap with the number and name of the regiment, the letter of the company, and the number of the soldier in black letters and figures.

## Another Enemy on the Same Battlefield

Doctors watched for any number of diseases or symptoms that could arise in a field hospital from the time a patient was first brought in or as he recovered from surgery.

Nurses and orderlies would check for the ugly and dreaded black spot, about the size of a dime, that could appear on a wound a few days after surgery. It was indicative of a literal rotting of the flesh as gangrene set in and contaminated the wound from the inside out.

By the time the wound took on a foul smell, the gangrene had likely spread so far that when it was detected, it was already too late, and doctors estimated that they lost 90 percent of these patients.

# The Number One Killer

Total estimates of Civil War deaths attribute 60 percent of Union and nearly 70 percent of Confederate mortality to disease.

## The Top Civil War Sharpshooter

The winner in this one, hands down, was "Sergeant Mosquito," a tiny adversary that used a very quick, short-range, .0002-caliber weapon to indiscriminately strike Union and Confederate soldiers in and around the many stagnant swamps of the South. Union estimates were that mosquitoes hit one million Northern soldiers and that one-fourth of all soldiers, both North and South, contracted malaria from this sharpshooting scourge.

## It's Enough to Make You Sick

As if bullets and mosquitoes weren't enough for Civil War soldiers to deal with, how about garbage? Tales of the horrible conditions in Confederate prison camps, where the same water was used for bathing and drinking, are common.

Camps were generally littered with trash, food, manure and even the remains of animals butchered to feed the troops.

Consequently, the most overwhelming statistic of the Civil War is the number of soldiers, North and South, who suffered from bowel disorders, diarrhea or dysentery—99.5 percent.

## Major Mortality

The Civil War killed more Americans than any other war we've ever fought.

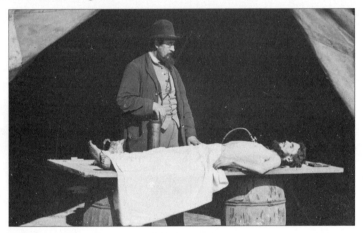

Embalming surgeon

# An Important New Profession

There were several new professions and refinements that came out of the Civil War, especially military inventions. What else? Why, embalming, of course. Embalming surgeons (they were doctors!) would set up shop near major troop encampments or near a sutler at a camp. Often they would contact the deceased's family, who would arrange to have their loved one embalmed so he could be shipped home via train or wagon to be buried without worrying that the body would decompose en route.

Embalming tent

The phenomenon, for whatever reason (likely simple economics, a lack of money to pay for the service, as well as a lack of doctors available in the South), only occurred in the North. There were few, if any, embalmers in the South.

The thousands of dead, North and South intermixed, on a battlefield made it difficult for an embalmer to find a particular body. And it was equally unlikely that the body he was looking for would be found intact. Officers were relatively easy to locate and identify, but the carnage on a battlefield made finding an enlisted man difficult or impossible.

### Camp and Outpost Duty for Infantry

The Commanding Officer of a Regiment is in the position of the father of a family; and it is his bounden duty to watch over the moral as well as the military conduct of those under his command.

# CELEBRATING THE WAR WITH A FAIR?

## Sanitary Fairs Were a Boon for Soldiers

Sanitary Commission, Washington, DC

✧

Sanitary Fairs, one of the most successful programs of the Civil War, were first privately run and then government supported. The speed and success with which the program operated was amazing. Comparable in some ways to the USO, Sanitary Fairs during the Civil War were a dramatically different and unique concept at the time. Their purpose was to raise funds, and what they did for soldiers, for their general well-being, their medical care and their continued survival, was exceptional.

The Sanitary Commission, which oversaw the entire process of these fairs and then translated the funds raised into actual products for soldiers' use in the field and for their care in hospitals was an astounding $4.814 million between June 1861 and July 1865. Some $4.531 million at least (we're not here to conduct an audit on the 150-year-old Sanitary Commission and will assume the remaining $283,000 was probably "inventory" of unused materials when the war ended, or even money in the bank that was later spent on goods for veterans) was spent in providing services directly to Union soldiers.

Although it's difficult to compare $4.5 million in 1860 to its value in the present, we can estimate what was provided with that money and what those items would cost in present-day currency. Those invaluable Sanitary Fairs raised money that bought clothing and other items for hundreds of thousands of soldiers, built hospitals as modern as others of the day, paid doctors and medical staff, purchased ambulances, wagons and even boats, paid thousands of staff salaries and much more. Today, salaries alone could be $200 million for the same services; construction of several hospitals would certainly cost $500 million today (it's incorrect to compare the cost of *those* hospitals today; instead, you must look at the cost of a comparably sized hospital operating today); and food, clothing and incidentals would conservatively cost $100 to $200 per soldier serving in the field and several times that for the men in hospital—or anywhere from $100 to $250 million more! In other words, while the cost of living index would not show it, just providing the soldiers with comparable resources 150 years later, the $4.5 million easily would need to be close to $1 billion today! That would be 222 times the "real" money the Sanitary Fairs raised during the Civil War. No doubt, the contemporary North, faced with the same challenges today, would probably create their own fairs, and in four years find a way to raise a billion dollars for the cause.

It's what people do when the need arises.

The Sanitary Commission was known by its public face at the Sanitary Fairs throughout the North that raised money for soldiers' needs and for the actual work that was done in the field—the delivery of an unprecedented volume of important goods to troops and field hospitals.

The hall of a Sanitary Fair

The Sanitary Fairs—the Great Midwestern Fair in Chicago, the Central Fair in Philadelphia and numerous others from Nantucket to New York—were held in both large and very modest-sized communities. Many fairs took place in town halls and pavilions, though some larger cities constructed complete buildings and courtyards for an event that would last just a few weeks.

Mothers, daughters, sisters and aunts contributed preserves, baked goods, clothing, quilts and many other items to be sold to the general public, with all the revenue going to purchase goods for the Union army. Donated items ranged from small

## Camp and Outpost Duty for Infantry

The outposts move to the support of the sentinels when attacked, forming as skirmishers.

pieces of pottery to world-class art. Lincoln provided his original copy of the Emancipation Proclamation; he and his cabinet also autographed documents to be sold. There were items that were easily purchased by those with minimal income to spare, and there were autographed items, household or office or personal effects from generals, politicians and notable citizens that were usually more expensive. At the Great Central Fair in Chicago, for example, a portrait of George Washington by Charles Willson Peale was donated (and sold) with a suggested value of $500! (Just as a side note, a Peale portrait of Washington sold for $21.3 million in 2005!)

Knowing that everything generated money for the troops and that all the funds were going to a worthy cause encouraged spending. The fact that the most famous people in the land were supportive in donating and buying made the fairs that much more successful. Fees for attendance ranged up to 50 cents per person, and "season tickets" for a fair's entire run could be purchased if a person wanted to attend every day. Communities supported the fairs en masse, with the result that entire hospitals and "halfway houses" for recovering wounded soldiers were built and staffed, and hundreds of wagonloads of goods were distributed to soldiers on the frontlines.

The Sanitary Fairs were a remarkable idea that became an even more remarkable success. The fairs and related donations brought in nearly $5 million total, and volunteers at each fair were repeatedly surprised by the public's generosity. Philadelphia's fair was planned, for example, with the goal of raising $25,000, but it brought in nearly six times that amount. The results were the same throughout the North.

### Keeping His Promise

Many of the Sanitary Commission volunteers handed out free paper, postage stamps and pens and ink to men in the hospitals, and they also often handed out religious literature. One day, an infantry soldier named Jack Boswell told a friend that a nice young woman had come around and offered a piece of fresh fruit to anyone who would accept Christian pamphlets. Boswell said that the pamphlet called dancing "the devil's work." He laughed aloud for several seconds and asked for a piece of fresh fruit, telling the young volunteer that he promised not to dance ever again. She was confused and wasn't sure what to say to him. Then he hiked up his bed-clothes and shook the stumps of his legs at her to show that although he'd lost them both, he still had his sense of humor.

## Don't Damage the Shiny New Hospital Supplies!

Hospital supplies were treasures, and one soldier incurred the wrath of a nurse and then a doctor from the Sanitary Commission when they discovered he had cut out a section of the new sheet on which he was lying. Customarily, Sanitary Commission workers wrote notes either on or in items that they packaged to be sent to hospitals, and on this particular sheet was written "Mary Evans, Salem, Mass. God bless the soldier who gets this. I shall pray for him every day." The soldier was so moved by the message that he cut it out from the sheet.

He had the piece of sheet he had cut out folded up in his hand and told the angry doctor that he would keep it with him all the rest of his days. The doctor just smiled and patted him on the arm, telling him not to worry about the sheet.

### Camp and Outpost Duty for Infantry

The officer should, under no circumstances, give way to a feel of despondency. When everything seems to be at the worst, then his greatest energies and skill should be called forth.

Zouave ambulance drill

cx/cx

# Ambulances that Were Probably Slow Enough to Catch

Military ambulances were used in one form or another from the beginning of the colonies, while they were fighting to become the United States. In the Revolutionary War, ambulances were simply covered wagons or litters available to haul wounded soldiers off the battlefield.

With casualties a thousand times higher in the Civil War, more than just a few wagons were necessary because thousands of soldiers were injured every day on the many battlefields. Union ambulance specifications were very complete. There was an ambulance corps, as well as specs for how ambulances of varying sizes should be built and equipped. Litters holding the wounded were supported on both sides of the ambulances, which were partitioned by curtains and had medical equipment, water jugs and other items in cabinets and on hooks inside.

Medical personnel in the field and those directing the war from Washington repeatedly stated that it was critical to treat battle injuries with the utmost speed. Once in hospitals, surgeries had to be performed quickly, but it was imperative that the injured be conveyed to field hospitals immediately—or there would be no patient on which to operate. There were myriad problems that could complicate a doctor's work, but just the loss of blood from injuries could take a life that otherwise might have been saved.

The *Nashville*, a riverboat converted to a Union hospital

## Union Ambulances—Not Just Wagons

Rivers often provided fast evacuation for injured troops. In many western battles, Northern wounded were evacuated by boat to cities in Illinois or directly to St. Louis, where large hospitals were available. And when the port city of Memphis on the Mississippi River fell relatively quickly in the war, that city became the site of a large hospital facility for Northern wounded.

## Evacuation by Rail as Well

Both North and South evacuated wounded via trains whenever they could. Although both sides would confiscate and use whatever was available as the fastest means of getting wounded to hospitals, the preference was always for passenger trains. Freight cars were far bumpier, dirtier and offered no furniture or carpeted floor for the wounded.

The unrelenting numbers of casualties meant that hospitals had to be provided somehow, somewhere. Surprisingly, the largest hospitals in the nation were two massive Confederate facilities in Richmond. Chimborazo, touted by the Confederacy as the largest such structure on the continent, had 8000 beds! The city's Jackson Hospital was nearly as large, with the ability to treat and house 6000 men.

The medical profession in both armies constructed pavilion-type hospitals, essentially a hub and spokes. The inner area housed operating rooms, the morgue, the kitchen and various other facilities, and the spokes were patient wings connected to the center by walkways or small wooden "streets" that would allow patient movement in chairs or on litters.

## Nutrition—In the Civil War?

Dr. Samuel Preston Moore was named the third Confederate Surgeon General just a few months into the Civil War. Almost everything in the South lagged sorrowfully behind the Union, and medical service, the number of doctors and nurses, and the availability of supplies were among the items on that list. The medical corps in the Confederate States of America relied on the state militia doctors and on the few physicians who resigned from the Union army to take similar posts for the Confederacy.

Moore was a strict disciplinarian, hardworking and anxious to have a well-run and modern military medical corps, which was a tad ambitious given the circumstances. He logically and accurately anticipated large numbers of casualties and demanded that the military develop plans to build large army hospitals—hospitals that would be clean, well ventilated and well stocked with drugs. He suggested several plans for nutrition as well, both for patients and for soldiers on active duty, even though there was little he could do to make it happen.

Moore went so far as to establish laboratories in the South that began manufacturing medicines and also distributing information on herbs and other plants found in the region that were said to have medicinal properties. Unfortunately, the U.S. naval blockade of Southern ports and a lack of funds in the Confederate Treasury combined to make most of Moore's plans moot.

Without ample funds, the South was short on hospital staff, beds and supplies throughout the war, and Moore's plans to import foreign medical supplies and medicines were effectively thwarted by the blockade.

## An Army Marches on Its Stomach

Even with the Sanitary Commission and fairs, Northern doctors faced similar problems to those in the South, just not as great or as widespread. On Sherman's March to the Sea, one would think that soldiers at the end of the war and at the end of a 300-mile march in worn-out shoes would be exhausted, hungry and unhealthy. But General William T. Sherman reported that his men were in the best condition of the war! *Why and how?* They managed to stay healthy and *well* fed because they had permission to forage en route, which meant taking chicken, eggs and whatever was at hand from private farms, often relieving their Southern "hosts" of bread, milk, meat, fruit and more.

## A Record to Be Proud Of

For all of 1862, the Washington, DC, Sanitary Commission House provided services and lodging for 8429 soldiers for a total of 22,698 nights, serving them a total of 55,810 meals. More than half of these men required medical assistance of some type, and were either treated on site or transferred to a local hospital. Of all the men who used the facility in that first year, only 11 died, those being so ill that they passed away before they could be transferred to a hospital.

The total cost of providing the care was quite low even in 1862 terms—less than $8000, or only 90 cents per man for his visit!—and those visits averaged more than 2.5 days each.

## Camp and Outpost Duty for Infantry

It is equally the duty of non-commissioned officers and soldiers, at all times and in all situations, to pay the proper compliments to officers of the navy and marines, and to officers of other regiments, when in uniform.

## Rules at Sanitary Commission Houses

1. No noisy talking or profane language.

2. Personal cleanliness must be observed.

3. All men who have a sum of money are advised to deposit it with the superintendent.

4. All men who are not seriously ill must be ready for breakfast at 6:00 AM, 7:00 AM in winter.

5. Any man who is intoxicated will be refused admission.

## From the Battlefield to Civilized Accommodations...Almost

In the dead of winter in Washington, DC, the Sanitary Commission was expecting 42 men from Harris' Light Cavalry and the 1st Vermont Cavalry. They were a mile and a half outside town because it was convenient to change horses there, which was not unusual. The sick soldiers were all in a single enclosed wagon by themselves.

First thing in the morning, Sanitary Commission volunteers took a wagon the short distance outside the city to "see what had become of the sick," according the facility director. "We found them all seated upon their knapsacks or lying upon their blankets on the ground. It seems the car in which the sick were left was needed and they were turned out" to huddle together in the weather until the wagon came to get them.

Fighting in disguise; Loreta Velazques as Harry Buford, Union soldier

## Daughters of the Regiment

Women known as Daughters of the Regiment were *not* prostitutes, the first question typically asked. They were women who lived in military camps, marched with the troops (often in uniform) and acted as nurses and friends (not lovers) to the troops. Twenty-year-old Eliza Wilson from Wisconsin was a typical Regimental Daughter. She dressed in a handsome uniform and had her own tent and even a personal servant, also a "camp follower" and not a soldier.

Wilson was attached to the 5th Wisconsin Volunteer Infantry, which included several of her relatives. The idea of Regimental Daughters grew out of the desire of sisters, cousins and even mothers and wives wanting to be near their family members.

Kady Brownwell was a "daughter" of three separate Rhode Island regiments; her husband fought in the 1st Rhode Island, one of the three. Once Brownwell and several other "daughters"—in their homemade uniforms that did not match official Union garb—were walking through a dense bit of forest near camp when a group of Union soldiers opened fire on what they took to be a small scout party of rebel soldiers. Fortunately, the first volleys hit no one, and Brownell raced to the front of the group carrying the regimental flag. Once the soldiers saw the Union banner, they ceased fire.

The stories of women who disguised themselves as men and actually fought in battle were hardly uncommon, though not ones you would hear every day. Many women in this situation worked in the North as spies and actually infiltrated Union regiments dressed as men.

## Camp and Outpost Duty for Infantry

All prisoners captured from the enemy will be turned over to the provost marshal of division, who will send them, at the earliest practicable moment...to the provost marshal general.

Sarah Edmonds, Union spy, dressed as Franklin Thompson

Sarah Edmonds was both a spy and a soldier, and many of her fellow company soldiers were shocked to hear that she wasn't Franklin Thompson, whom she continued to portray for years after the war. In the 1880s, she contacted soldiers to attest to her service in an effort to obtain a pension. They were in disbelief that their friend, a male nurse in the 2nd Michigan Volunteers, was actually a woman. She impressed other soldiers with her shooting and riding skills, as she had learned to do both growing up. Soldiers often washed with just a splash from a basin and stayed in their clothes around the clock out of necessity—they had nowhere to bathe and no clean clothes…and battle could be at hand at any moment. Consequently, it was not difficult to hide her identity.

Yet another female soldier was Fanny Wilson of New Jersey, who fought for the Union army for 18 months. Her identity was discovered when she was wounded at Vicksburg.

Amy Clark was a Confederate soldier who had joined to be near her husband, but after he was killed in battle, she continued to fight in the war.

## Camp and Outpost Duty for Infantry

If from any wound the blood spirts out in jets instead of a steady stream, you will die in a few minutes unless it be remedied, because an artery has been divided, and that takes the blood direct from the fountain of life.

Jennie Hodgers fought in an Illinois regiment as Albert Cashier for four years and decided to keep her male disguise after the war. Her real identity was only found out when she was in an automobile accident—nearly 50 years later, in 1911.

Numerous women were more than content to retain their female roles, working as spies to infiltrate one side or the other to gain information. Many ended up in prison, where most were treated with leniency, the exception being those who plotted directly to harm the other side. Much was made of the fact that one of the convicted conspirators in the assassination of Lincoln was a woman, Mary Surrat. She earned a place on the gallows remarkably quickly and was hanged along with the others who were convicted in what generally was acknowledged to be a very fast trial with preconceived notions about who was guilty.

## Louisa May Alcott

Alcott's name has been known for generations, primarily by young female readers. The author wrote dozens of books, none more popular than *Little Women*, an autobiographical novel of four sisters coming of age in New England during the Civil War. She was a staunch abolitionist and champion of women's rights.

### Camp and Outpost Duty for Infantry

It will seldom happen, in an action, that the supply of ammunition carried by the men will be exhausted before the regiment will be temporarily relieved. If such should be the case, however, the men will not leave the ranks, but notify the file-closers that their supply is getting low.

# JUST FINDING ONESELF WAS DIFFICULT

*Every story about the Civil War seems replete with so many ways to suffer and even more ways to die. A quick death on the battlefield came to many, but the pain and anguish of being wounded was often better than the slow, lingering death in a prisoner-of-war camp. Being locked in a Civil War prison was often a death sentence. There were too many ways to die, and an awful lot of ways simply to disappear.*

## Civil War Headquarters in Cairo?

What Civil War leader had his headquarters in Cairo? Earlier in history, it might have been Ramses, Alexander the Great or Ptolemy, but during the U.S. Civil War, it was, of course, General Ulysses S. Grant. The general established his headquarters in 1861 in Cairo, Illinois—the county seat of, well, no surprise, Alexander County.

During the war, Cairo was strategically important as both a Union supply point and a training center. The city is at the confluence of the Mississippi and the Ohio rivers at the southernmost tip of the state.

## Southern Records Lost in the Siege of Richmond

The total number of men who fought and died in the Civil War is all estimates, quite accurate from the Union perspective and nearly all speculation on the Confederate side. The bound set of records of the War of the Rebellion looks like a dozen sets of encyclopedias on a shelf—literally millions of pages of reports, requisitions, orders and subordinate documents. If you were to put together all the photographic records, regimental histories, diaries and firsthand accounts of the war that were actually published as books just in the first few years after the war, you would have an entire library in itself—a library that might fill several rooms with floor-to-ceiling shelving. The North was en route to an obvious victory, and when it became equally obvious that Richmond was certain to fall, Confederate leaders removed or burned ultra-sensitive documents. When Union troops moved in, they virtually destroyed the city and set it aglow. The seat of the Confederate government, the masses of records, the broad history of the war from the South's perspective and many Southern records were destroyed in their entirety. In a moment's victory, so much history was set ablaze and lost forever.

The loss made every Civil War historian's job not just more difficult, but impossible on many levels. How many Confederates served here? How many were killed there? And how many were lost or wounded at this battle? After Richmond burned, it was rebuilt, as was Atlanta and myriad small towns across America. But how many soldiers' heroics, how many battles and how many records were lost? No one will ever know, but entire buildings holding records about secession and the subsequent battles went up in flames.

Besides those endless volumes of government and military records, there is the entirely separate issue of documenting the Civil War from the Confederate point of view. Union correspondence, from soldiers to home and vice versa, was aided immeasurably by the Sanitary Commission, without which

## Camp and Outpost Duty for Infantry

Courtesy among military men is indispensable to discipline.

only a fraction of the letters would have been written; there was nothing similar in the South. Also in the South, literacy lagged well behind the North, certainly affecting the volume of personal correspondence. The number of diaries was a fraction of those written in the North, and diaries, personal accounts and regimental histories were also primarily a Northern product. Printing and publishing books was nearly a totally Northern industry, something that no doubt affected this aspect of recollections and important stories of the war.

The combination of all the Confederate States' and military records being burned and the dramatically lower number of personal accounts in letters, diaries and books in the South means that the most-written-about war in history is viewed predominantly from the North's perspective.

## Counting the Cost

The loss of records in Richmond becomes almost irrelevant when examining other battle, skirmish, cemetery, hospital and enlistment records. Just the estimated numbers are staggering. The single largest statistic: deaths. More than 600,000 men—North and South—were killed in battle or died as a result of injuries, diseases, drownings or other miscellaneous causes such as imprisonment. Union figures are solid, based on accurate (or nearly so!) records, whereas Confederate numbers are largely estimates.

For every 1000 Union soldiers who went into battle, Northern army records say 112—or 11.2 percent—were wounded or killed. Put in perspective, a soldier lined up with his 100-man company, 50 to the left, 50 to the right, and when the battle was over, 11 of those men (one in every nine) had fallen.

In the South, the numbers were not perfectly accurate, but they were very good estimates compiled long after the war and after hundreds of statisticians, soldiers and historians

Graves at City Point, Virginia

had examined every aspect of the conflict under a microscope. A comparable 100-man company of rebels, marching to face their opposite numbers, saw a third more fall. Fifteen out of that 100—or 15 percent—of every Southern company was lost to injury or death.

Heroes were made in every battle; brave men with no medals fell at every juncture in the war. So many were forgotten and, worse, many lost their lives and their families never knew where or how. But the heroes of the war, men and women, also included those who spent their lives looking for the lost.

## An Army of Volunteers

The Union army was known as an "army of volunteers" in the country, in the press and throughout history. It is a well-known fact that most of those who went to war were, indeed, volunteers, but there was also a draft, which was used to fill the ranks whenever the numbers of soldiers needed soared. The army's need for men was huge, but volunteers supplemented the draft, often with 100-percent local volunteer units.

There was an obvious hope, from Lincoln down to company commanders, that there would be a balance between volunteers and "regular army" troops—that the regular army in place when the war began would be the glue that held the units together. But the number of enlisted men was a mere fraction of what was needed to start the war, and a staggeringly small number of those were still alive when the conflict ended four years later.

Early in the war, the Union was already experiencing much greater casualties than they anticipated. General McClellan, for example, had 158,000 under his command in February 1862 and only 5000 (or a little over three percent) were regular army—the rest were draftees or volunteers! And if one considered that most officers were *not* volunteers, it was an uncomfortable thought for a general to be facing battle with 5000 men familiar with the military and 153,000 who were not!

Continuity was lacking everywhere. When McClellan took charge of the Army of the Potomac, he reported that he was shocked at what he found, beyond simply inexperienced infantry. He desperately needed trained men for both the cavalry and artillery as he looked forward at the potential battles in the coming months.

### Camp and Outpost Duty for Infantry

If animals about camp are to be shot, they will, under orders from quarter-master, be taken to the side of a trench already prepared, and thrown in and covered up as soon as dead.

# DEATH COMES CALLING

## Death in Battle, by Sunstroke and by Suicide

Beyond the astounding numbers of men wounded or killed in battle, the numbers who died through other means is just as incredible today as it was to the generals—and to Abraham Lincoln—at the time.

More than 14,000 deaths are classified as, well, "unclassified" by the army and the government of the United States. This is to say that they were not combat deaths, but rather deaths within the military, and those could occur in so many ways, unfortunately. Wounded men died. Captured men died. Healthy men quickly became unhealthy, and many of the sick died. Prisoners of war died awful, pitiful deaths in Southern camps, regardless of their health when captured. These deaths were not classified as battle mortality but were clearly caused by the war.

Beyond these Union soldiers, sailors and marines who died non-combat deaths, how do we even begin to categorize civilian deaths in the war? They were *not* measured by the military, and thus were not measured at all.

Countless civilians were killed by military fire (or military fires!); slaves were killed by their former owners and by roving bands of vigilantes or even by accidental combat fire; and myriad other Northerners and Southerners—Americans— died as "collateral damage." In the Civil War era, these deaths were not just unclassified but unrecorded, and the numbers in the North were a fraction of those in the South.

How many thousands of residents of Atlanta or Richmond or the numerous small towns in the path of the war, black and white, male and female, adults and children, were killed when their homes were overrun by battles or when Sherman burned them? For every recorded non-military death, how many unnamed Southerners also simply ceased to exist?

And although so many of the South's records were lost, we have copious Union records. For example, of the more than 14,000 unclassified Union forces' deaths, almost 5000 of those were soldiers and sailors who drowned during their military service in the Civil War! Another 313 died from sunstroke and 391—perhaps a small number considering the conditions—committed suicide. And 4200 deaths are listed simply as "accidental." If anyone knew about those accidents, nothing was ever recorded, and those stories—sad, wild, crazy or perhaps unbelievable—are forever lost.

## A Last-minute Reprieve

In an attack on Yorktown in 1861, Private William Scott of Company K was among those from the Virginia 4th and 6th of the Union army responsible for picket duty while his comrades ate and rested. He fell asleep and, of course, by doing so endangered all the men. The penalty for falling asleep at your post as a picket? Death by firing squad.

The honorable, patriotic soldier accepted his fate, but some-one in his unit contacted President Lincoln, extolling the virtues of the young man, acknowledging his mistake and begging the president to pardon him, which Lincoln did! This is quite amazing considering the chaos of war and the postal system of the time, but then, access to the president was much less difficult when compared to the world today.

Mr. Lincoln was apparently so concerned about the rapid timeline for executions that he feared young Scott might die before word of his pardon reached the unit commander. Further demonstrating Lincoln's humanity and concern for others, the president called for a carriage to take him personally

Federal pickets outside Atlanta, Georgia

the 10 miles south from Washington, DC, to the battle lines in Virginia to ensure that his pardon reached the young soldier before his own troops carried out the death sentence. President Lincoln arrived in time, met the soldier he had saved and others on the front line, then returned to the city.

Soon thereafter, Company K went into battle again. This time, Scott was not on picket duty, but on the frontlines when his unit engaged Confederate troops. Private Scott was hit six times by rifle fire and mortally wounded. He was comforted by a friend in the company and, with literally his dying breath as he lay on the battlefield, Scott said, "Bless the president for believing in me."

## December 21, 1864

General Sherman captures the city of Savannah, Georgia, the culmination of his destructive "March to the Sea."

## The Most Despised Southerner

Andersonville Prison was far and away the most notorious of all the Southern prisoner-of-war camps. It was the most overcrowded, the filthiest and the largest. Just approaching a stockade wall was ample reason for shots to ring out, and prisoners, without warning, were sometimes shot dead.

Captain Henry Wirz was commander of the facility, and he was arrested immediately at the end of the war and tried for a list of crimes against humanity. The charges against him were explicit, unlike many other vague accusations in which the camp or environment seemed to be on trial rather than a specific individual. Wirz was charged, promptly convicted and subsequently executed for the following crimes:

1.  Deaths of Union prisoners resulting from mutilation by hounds

2.  Deaths of Union prisoners resulting from confinement in the stocks and on the chain gang

3.  Deaths of Union prisoners by guards under direct orders from Wirz

4.  Direct deaths of Union prisoners by Wirz's own hand.

### Camp and Outpost Duty for Infantry

Pickets move forward to the outposts, or the outposts and sentinels, skirmishing, retire slowly on the pickets, as the nature and force of the attack, or the orders from commanding officers may direct.

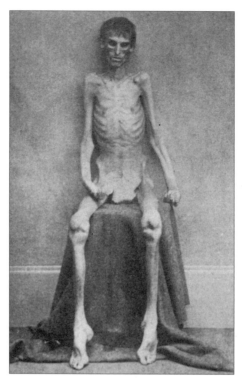

A Federal prisoner after his release from prison

## The Bell Isle Rather than the South Beach Diet

The camp at Belle Island in Richmond was like virtually all Confederate prisons: overcrowded, understaffed and painfully lacking in even the most basic necessities of life—it was as bad as most in the Confederacy.

Union prisoners' daily allocation of food was a handful of corn and a spoonful of beans. Drinking water came from the same limited source that was used for bathing and often for sewage. When Belle Island was liberated at the end of the war, the fabulous Bell Isle diet had worked wonders: nine out of 10 prisoners weighed less than 100 pounds.

## Being Captured Might Almost Be a Good Thing

After being captured, Confederate prisoners were generally treated quite a great deal better than Union prisoners, but then, not all Union troops were subjected to the horrific circumstances at places such as Andersonville, either. All prisoners were forced to travel light—very light—with just whatever they had on their person, less weapons and ammunition. Depending on where soldiers were captured, they could have a long, long march or perhaps be just 15 or 16 miles from their destination.

Generally, the first Confederate meal fed to Union prisoners lacked imagination, but if they were lucky, there was enough substance to fill their bellies. The rebels gave their prisoners cornmeal and salt beef (salted and dried, it was a very tough and a not-very-tasty version of beef jerky). The soldiers were allowed to build fires, and they mixed the cornmeal with water on a rubber blanket, then spread it on a board and baked it in the campfire with a little salt chipped from the salt beef. The food looked bad, but after the soldiers had been in prison for a while and lacked anything edible, their first meals as prisoners of war began to look better and better.

### Camp and Outpost Duty for Infantry

The line of pickets should be located with a view to the most extensive observation possible of the country in front.

## Camp Ford—No Southern Comfort

Every prison was different. At a gathering some 20-plus years after the war, one soldier told veterans from his unit of his capture and incarceration at Camp Ford, near Tyler, Texas. The prison might have been better than some, but was probably not quite the Hilton of the South. The prison camp covered seven acres, but four acres had been recently logged and were open. The camp itself, an enclosed stockade, covered three acres. The fence was made of heavy split timbers—no one was going to go over or through it.

There were cabins (for officers only), while enlisted men had to dig pits out of the hard clay in which to sleep, sharing the work and digging pits for two or three men to share. There was plenty of free time, but there was an urgency to make a place to sleep and to find a place to stay dry or cool, depending on the location.

Prisoners at Camp Ford were treated immeasurably better than their counterparts in other camps; they were given permission to go out of the stockade (under guard) to pull or knock down small trees or, in rare cases, to cut whatever wood they could with pocketknives to build their own shelters; they were not given axes or saws or sets of blueprints for a log cabin, but they were given access to what the camp lacked—the armfuls of branches and scrap bits of trees amounted to a king's ransom of building materials. The best prisoner-built structures were made of grass, poles and shrubs, but a roof overhead was luxury in a Confederate prison.

Camp Ford prison inmates also had the luxury of fresh beef on occasion, as cattle wandered the field outside the prisoners' enclosure. When the prison guards and Confederate troops had fresh beef, so did the prisoners, which may have been a unique circumstance compared to all the other Confederate prisons.

Many of the men were nearly nude, their uniforms in tatters from being worn 24 hours a day, and unprotected in the hot Texas sun. When the weather turned cold, the Confederate guards, who also hardly had quality supplies for themselves, decided (unlike so many others) "to play by the rules" and pass on the Sanitary Commission and Union army supplies sent for the prisoners, plus what one inmate remembers as clearly Confederate clothes. There were 1500 suits of clothing and a similar number of blankets.

One of the toughest tasks in any prison camp was cooking, even just boiling water. In some instances, guards, after they had cooked during the day, would loan their pans to inmates to cook or boil water in the evening or during the night.

Inside the camps or outside the compound, valuable "finds" for prisoners were cow horns, a rare commodity that was used for carving. The men played chess or checkers as a diversion during the long, long days with little to do. The chess or checker sets were carved out of whatever the men could find and, again, they had time, time and more time. Some even tried growing a vegetable garden, with minor success. Water for drinking, washing and the garden came from a spring in the corner of the enclosure.

Typical of all prisoner-of-war camps in the South, Union troops saw no mail for months. After soldiers had been in prison long enough that their whereabouts were known, mail would trickle in, once a month, at best.

The guards were anxious to trade Confederate dollars for U.S. greenbacks. At the beginning of 1864, 10 Confederate dollars were the equivalent of one U.S. dollar; over the next nine or 10 months, the exchange rate rose steadily to 20, 40, and then 60 Confederate dollars for one U.S. dollar. By the time the prisoners were released in early 1865, Confederate dollars had no value whatsoever. Shoes would have been a more valuable currency.

Once the war ended, the prisoners were on their own and could either wait for Union troops or develop their own plan for making a trek North or to a river where they might gain passage. The closest way home from the Texas prison was a march of more than 100 miles to the nearest port, where they might find a Union garrison and book passage on a riverboat headed north out of Texas.

## Camp and Outpost Duty for Infantry

Regimental quartermasters will see that their teamsters understand how to take the wagons apart and put them together.

# At Salisbury Prison

Southern prisons have always been viewed as being akin to the wretched camp at Andersonville. But while it's a fact that most Union troops captured and imprisoned in the South suffered terribly, some did so only because of the lack of facilities, not because of vicious staff whose primary mission was to starve or otherwise make the prisoners suffer. Often the food and poor hygiene were enough to kill the starving inmates without any intent whatsoever.

The former factory at Salisbury in North Carolina opened as a prison at the end of 1861, and in less than six months, housed 1400 Union POWs. It had a four-story brick building and numerous small structures. Food and water were more than adequate, the prison was uncharacteristically roomy and the prisoners played baseball, performed in plays and carved items to pass the time. One could almost call it a model Civil War prison early in the war.

After a prisoner exchange, Salisbury was nearly empty, and the facility built to house 2500 was a ghost town of some 16 acres by 1864. But the war was raging, and seemingly overnight, 9000 Union troops were packed into the site. Rations were inadequate, water scarce, sewage backed up, vermin everywhere, no heating fuel and men were housed in tents where baseball fields formerly filled the prison yard. Suddenly, 20 men a day were dying.

Many attempted to escape, typically by tunneling under the fence surrounding the prison. But in November 1864, hundreds of prisoners rushed the gates, took weapons from the guards and broke toward the woods. The guards fought back, firing a cannon at the weak prisoners, who had no chance.

In the almost $3^1/_2$ years that Salisbury Prison was open, it held some 15,000 prisoners—4000 of whom died there.

## Northern Newspapermen Escape Rebel Prison

Several Northern newspapermen, including Messieurs Richardson and Davis from Cincinnati and New York, were arrested and jailed in a military prison in North Carolina. They were periodically allowed to leave the main prison enclosure to carry medical supplies to the prison hospital.

Their escape plan required "sharing" passes. First, the two men left with their passes, having shown them to the guard, who allowed them to leave the prison to pick up medical supplies for the hospital. However, only one man returned, showing his pass and reentering the prison. Meanwhile, the second man hid in a storage shed between the hospital and the prison.

Later in the day, two men left again—the prisoner who had gone on the hospital pickup earlier and a third man—using the same two passes. The guard recognized the passes and the men's faces but not their names, as he apparently couldn't read or recall which person went with what name. He let both men leave the prison to carry more goods to the hospital. They carried some boxes into the hospital and then left, joining the man who was hiding in the shed instead of returning to the prison enclosure. With thousands of prisoners inside the walls, no one missed the three who never came back.

After dark, the three men slipped into the hospital. No one questioned them because they were there often. Then all three simply walked out into the town from the other side of the hospital, where guards assumed they were medical staff so did not stop them. The fact that they were dressed in decent civilian clothes and did not have the haggard or diseased appearance of prisoners meant that they were ignored once they left the hospital. Although the details are not specific, the fugitives reported that they found their way to the North immediately after their escape, which probably was never even noticed by the prison officials.

## Camp and Outpost Duty for Infantry

Fatigue parties will be frequently employed in removing and covering the filth, which, notwithstanding these regulations, may have so accumulated as to render parts of the camp offensive; and if the quarters of any particular corps be found dirty, some restraint or additional fatigue duties will be imposed on that regiment.

## Civil War Machine Gun—Sort Of

The very famous Gatling gun is often associated with the Civil War—incorrectly. The gun was developed before the war, patented in 1862 and tested during the war, but only a few were in use before 1865, and the weapon was not a factor in the Civil War.

The gun was developed by Dr. Richard Jordan Gatling, and the Civil War was considered a testing ground and provided an opportunity to work out several "bugs" so that it could be put into use after the war. Apparently, no one saw the dramatic possibilities had the guns been rushed to Union troops.

The Gatling gun has often mistakenly been called a machine gun, but it is a manually operated weapon with six barrels synchronized so that one fires while the others are cooled. The automatic feeding of the rifle bullets and a crank to rotate the barrels allow it to be fired at what feels like machine-gun speed compared to a single-shot rifle. Reports during a Civil War test noted that the gun could fire 150 shots per minute "and continue for hours without danger" of over-heating. Gatling listed his gun as able to fire significantly faster, as well. The value of the weapon was obvious, and had it made its full manufacturing debut earlier and been a part of the Union artillery in great numbers, the war would no doubt have gone dramatically faster. A two-man team firing 150 rounds per minute versus 150 men firing the same number with less accuracy offers an amazing contrast.

One would think that the Union army would have been so impressed in tests that they would have urged the final testing and delivery of hundreds of guns, which certainly would have ended many bloody battles much quicker and with dramatically fewer deaths on the Union side. A row of Gatlings replacing a regiment of men could have mowed down the enemy faster

### Andersonville Prison:

The most notorious of all Civil War prisons was the Confederate hell known as Andersonville. Initially built as a 16-acre stockade to hold up to 10,000 prisoners, 10 acres were added to accommodate more prisoners, and within six months of opening, 30,000 Union prisoners of war were crammed inside. Poor sanitation, crowding, minimal food and sweltering summer heat combined with often-cruel guards and an equally cruel commander (Captain Henry Wirz, who was tried, convicted and executed for war crimes immediately after the war) resulted in 13,000 deaths at the camp in one year—almost one-third of the 40,000 men held there the year the prison opened.

than hundreds, perhaps thousands, of soldiers. Either Gatling never pressed hard enough or the word never moved through channels fast enough to have the gun used in battle.

General Benjamin Butler purchased a dozen Gatling guns from the manufacturer at a reputed price of $1000 per gun and put them into service very briefly before the war ended, testing them both on land and on the deck of a gunboat. And that was the extent of the weapon's use in the Civil War.

## Civil War Math: .44 + .36 = 335,000

By far the biggest weapons producer in the Civil War was Samuel Colt's Connecticut factory, which produced handguns for both the Union army and navy.

For the war, Colt produced 150,000 of its .44-caliber Army pistols, the vast majority of which were sold to the army, and 185,000 .36-caliber revolvers for the navy. The weapons were produced well before the war started, and many were purchased by private individuals in the South and became the preferred side arm of Confederate horse soldiers.

The federal government also purchased more than 100,000 Remington revolvers during the war, paying $12 per gun, or about half of what Colt's weapons cost. At the end of the war, discharged soldiers were given the opportunity to purchase their side arms, and while cost may have been a major issue, Remingtons still outsold Colts, the assumption being that they were simply cheaper and at least as good as a Colt.

The list of rifle manufacturers was lengthy, and throughout the war, refinements and changes to guns were often made. Accuracy and speed were logically the major factors. Brands purchased by the Union for its soldiers—and in many cases used by the South after the weapons were captured in battle—included Sharps, Enfields (British), the Henry (noted for carrying 16 shots!), Spencers, Springfields and the Austrian-manufactured Lorenz, a popular purchase by the U.S. government.

Confederates were consistently short of weapons and manufacturing materials. Several efforts were made to copy U.S. Colts and other guns, but their available materials were generally poor.

One interesting factory, Griswold and Gunnison, near Macon, Georgia, had two dozen employees making copies of the navy's .36-caliber Colts called "Griswolds." They produced some 3600 pistols for the Confederate army in a plant where all but two workers were slaves.

## April 2, 1865

The Confederates evacuate Richmond, Virginia.

# Bayonets: Cooking Utensils or Weapons?

The general consensus in the Civil War was that the bayonet was as much a "tool" as an implement of war. Injuries and deaths from bayonets were near the bottom of the list of Civil War casualties.

Soldiers used rifles with bayonets attached as posts to support their tents (with the bayonet securely stuck in the ground) and in different configurations to hold up a lean-to or two-man tent, to hold meat over the fire and for raising signals or flags high enough so they could be seen.

### Camp and Outpost Duty for Infantry

No honors are paid by troops on the march or at halts.

# THE AFTEREFFECTS OF THE WAR LASTED FOR DECADES

*The period that immediately followed the end of official hostilities was known as Reconstruction. That meant the rebuilding of the South, its infrastructure and its economy. But what of the lives, the social aspects and the region's economy, which had been based on cotton, tobacco and slavery since the colonies won their independence from England? And what about rebuilding lives? While the North was in much better shape by comparison, reconstruction was necessary there, too.*

## Surrender at the Appomattox Court House

One Union soldier who watched the events of the day wrote in a letter to his cousin what transpired as troops were at rest and cavalry dismounted, and Robert E. Lee, still upright, strong and proud, left his horse with a soldier outside the courthouse. The soldier watched what took place before and after:

> "General Custer sent [Lee] word that it must be 'unconditional surrender.' They drew up on a hill about one mile from Appomattox Court House. General Sheridan came up, and he and General Lee went into the little

### Camp and Outpost Duty for Infantry

All inferiors are required to obey strictly, and to execute with alacrity and good faith, the lawful orders of the superiors appointed over them.

house, and General Grant was sent for as he was not far away. I went over to the rebel camp in the PM, and had a chat with our Southern brethren, most of whom were glad of the doings of the day."

There was no doubt in anyone's mind that the surrender was unconditional, but perhaps the arrogant Custer might be the one man who would tell Lee what he already knew. If that happened a mile up the small hill from the courthouse, our observer was also fleet afoot in hearing remarks on the hill— and then at the "small building" that the officers entered.

Custer romped through his Civil War tenure with the occasional reprimand and a reputation as an adequate soldier, but one prone to acting well before thinking. Naturally, that reputation later took him to his grave and forever ensured his place in history, dubious as it was, whereas his reputation as a Civil War officer would hardly have warranted much discussion. Custer finished last in his class at West Point, but he worked his way up the ranks, often successful in battle but equally often annoying superior officers. When the war ended, for some reason he occupied a prominent position outside Appomattox Court House (one wonders if it was merely a coincidence, but Custer never seemed to be in any position that he wasn't strongly involved in selecting), where he became the general who accepted the surrender flag from perhaps the finest general and gentleman of the war, Robert E. Lee.

Even the most elementary Civil War historians and students know that the war ended with the signing of the South's surrender inside Appomattox Court House in Virginia, where Lee surrendered his forces officially to his Union counterpart and future president, General Ulysses S. Grant. The generals sat at separate tables to sign the documents, surrounded by the high-ranking officers of each army.

Although they spoke little once inside, Lee asked Grant to allow Confederate soldiers to retain their horses and their rifles, which in virtually all cases they brought to the war with them. Side arms were to be laid down and taken up by the Union army.

Lincoln, of course, issued his famous pardon of all men who fought for the Confederacy, effective immediately with Lee's surrender, thus ensuring that no one could be tried for treason for having fought against the Union.

Destroyed houses, Fredericksburg, Virginia, 1862

## Measuring What Was Needed

The Civil War tore apart families and friends, cities and towns, and the existing social structure. Atlanta, Richmond and other towns few have heard of were nearly or mostly destroyed. Many things, from entire plantations and their crops to government records, simply ceased to exist in the South along with countless aspects of life. Psychological and structural reconstruction was as large a task as restoring legal and social order.

The Civil War showed military forces all over the world what could be expected of and done with ironclad warships. Flamethrowers, landmines and repeating rifles were all part of the Civil War legacy.

Besides modernized weapons and dramatic new ways to kill more efficiently, the Civil War also gave us non-military "firsts." What we think of them is also a matter for future debate. Thanks to the war, the country had its first tobacco tax. Lest we feel that the Northerners missed out, *all* Americans were blessed with a new and everlasting thing called the Federal Income Tax.

## The Summer of '65 in Louisiana

With the war over, representatives in many capacities from the United States government began working to help myriad causes in the South. The newly formed Freedmen's Bureau had a single goal and a single clientele to serve: former slaves. The organization's name was a bit of a misnomer, but it was the 19th century, after all. It was indeed a freed people's (ex-slaves') organization. The Freedmen's Bureau was formed to help settle slaves—men, women and children—in the North as well as the South, if they wanted to stay. The Bureau established schools and agency offices where former slaves could be coached and given guidance in finding work, what they might be paid, where to live in the North, how to adjust, where to find housing and schooling and so much more.

Agents of the Bureau in the South were met with indifference on one end of the spectrum and hate and threats on the other. Many in the South felt that their lives had been taken and their entire social structure stripped clean. They had lived the plantation life, as overseers and fence builders, repairmen and farmhands. As farm and plantation owners, they relied on their slaves for all aspects of their lives. Many were resigned to the losses of the war and the changes it brought, but from the coming Reconstruction all the way through to the Civil Rights movement nearly 90 years later, violence and hatred continued in the South. But slaves and now free black men, women and children saw change every day and had won something that the evils of the South could not take away—their freedom.

One Freedmen's Bureau agent began surveying his new position in the South and came face to face with a broadside posted for the benefit of the newly freed slaves on a plantation. The agent took it down and crumpled it up. The poster, labeled "Proclamation," read:

> "I have been a kind master, as my father was before me. I have fed, clothed, sheltered and cared for you. Whoever stays with me will get honest pay for his work. You have to take orders from me, and there is to be no more foolishness in the future about your working than there has been in the past. On this place I am always master, yet always your friend."

It was a bit ironic that the plantation owner chose to post the flyer, since none of his slaves could read and were, in fact, forbidden to learn while they were slaves. It was illegal in the South to teach a slave to read, with harsh penalties for anyone foolish enough to do so.

### Camp and Outpost Duty for Infantry

The brigade surgeon will frequently inspect the policing, cooking, clothing, and cleanliness of the camps; the position and condition of the sinks, the drainage and ventilation of the tents.

## The Merry Old Month of May in Texas

When word spread that Lee had surrendered and the war was over, it naturally took days, even weeks, to notify troops throughout the South. Desertion rates were already high, and several generals in charge of Confederate troops in three states—Texas, Louisiana and Arkansas—vowed to fight on despite the surrender. In Texas, the word was out by the last week of April, but May was hell.

Troops in Galveston mutinied but were coaxed back by their officers. Civilians began looting and stealing, including a complete ravaging of the blockade-runner *Lark*. Houston's ordnance building was sacked and so was the clothing bureau; there were riots throughout that Texas city and many others, with deaths at each riot. The state treasury building in Austin was raided and $17,000 in gold taken. Much of Texas was completely lawless; fewer than half the estimated 60,000 troops in the state remained on military duty.

The war had been over for a month by the time the last Confederate units went home, but the general lawlessness continued until the arrival of Union—that is, U.S.—troops, and the rebuilding of the South began in very small steps.

## The Worst Accident

The war was finally over and hundreds of thousands of men had been laid to rest. In what should have been a time of relief and recuperation, death came calling yet again. The worst accident in Civil War history—in all of U.S. maritime history—took place on April 27, 1865, when the steamboat paddlewheeler SS *Sultana* sank in the muddy Mississippi River seven miles north of Memphis. The ship was over-loaded with Union soldiers who had been released from Confederate POW prisons and was taking them home, a fact that seems to amplify the tragedy.

Reconstruction began the moment Lincoln declared that the people of the North and South were reunited and were again a single country. There would be no animosity, just rebuild-ing. The levels of pain in millions of hearts could hardly be measured—the loss of fathers and brothers, aunts and uncles and children, the loss of homes and belongings. It would not be easy to rebuild, but at least a start had been made.

For the families of the 2300 returning prisoners of war aboard the *Sultana*, joy was short-lived. First one, then another of the ship's boilers exploded. The captain, most of the crew and 1400 to 1800 Union prison camp survivors were killed in the explosion and fire. Hundreds more died of their wounds in hospital.

The ship was clearly licensed to carry only *up to* 365 passengers, but the Union needed ships to bring soldiers and prisoners of war home, so they contracted with private companies and clearly took them at their word. When asked how many men the *Sultana* could transport safely, the company replied, coincidentally, the same number waiting to go home: 2300. It was the worst maritime disaster at the time, and a century and a half later, fortunately, the record remains unsurpassed.

## Final Resting Place

Tens of thousands of war dead were buried where or close to where they fell. Makeshift cemeteries cropped up like new cornfields wherever the Union and Confederate troops did battle.

Unfortunately, haste in withdrawing or pursuing meant that many bodies were left where they fell. Those that could be identified—if time permitted—were put in a decently marked grave. When troops had time, they often buried the battle dead in graves marked simply with the number of unknown Union or Confederate soldiers.

Scores of volunteers combed the battle sites after the war in an attempt to identify the remains of soldiers from both sides and to rebury them with proper honors. Cemeteries became permanent neighbors to battlefields from the beginning of the war in many places, and long afterward in others.

Dead soldiers in trenches after battle

The dedication of the overwhelmingly large Gettysburg National Cemetery took place surprisingly soon after the battle, long before the war was over. Perhaps it was fitting that the battle was such a turning point only halfway through the war. It was there, of course, just over four months after the battle, that President Lincoln was called on to make what were described as "a few appropriate remarks" during the dedication of the new cemetery. Lincoln was sure his comments were inconsequential, but the Battle of Gettysburg would be remembered for decades, perhaps centuries to come, as would the president's Gettysburg Address.

## Camp and Outpost Duty for Infantry

The amount of weight to be carried in each wagon will usually be prescribed. The wagons should on no account whatever be overloaded. This is of great importance.

# Lincoln's Gettysburg Address

"Four score and seven years ago our fathers brought forth on this continent, a new nation, conceived in Liberty, and dedicated to the proposition that all men are created equal.

Now we are engaged in a great civil war, testing whether that nation, or any nation so conceived and so dedicated, can long endure. We are met on a great battle-field of that war. We have come to dedicate a portion of that field, as a final resting place for those who here gave their lives that that nation might live. It is altogether fitting and proper that we should do this.

But, in a larger sense, we can not dedicate—we can not consecrate—we can not hallow—this ground. The brave men, living and dead, who struggled here, have consecrated it, far above our poor power to add or detract. The world will little note, nor long remember what we say here, but it can never forget what they did here. It is for us the living, rather, to be dedicated here to the unfinished work which they who fought here have thus far so nobly advanced. It is rather for us to be here dedicated to the great task remaining before us—that from these honored dead we take increased devotion to that cause for which they gave the last full measure of devotion—that we here highly resolve that these dead shall not

## Camp and Outpost Duty for Infantry

During an action the men are not to leave the ranks, either for ammunition or to assist the wounded, unless by special directions. The ammunition will be received from quarter-masters, through the quarter-master's sergeants, by the 3rd sergeants of companies, and by them distributed. The wounded will be cared for by the hospital attendants and bands especially detailed for that purpose.

have died in vain—that this nation, under God, shall have a new birth of freedom—and that government of the people, by the people, for the people, shall not perish from the earth."

## Unknown Soldiers

Modern records note that more than 300,000 Civil War soldiers are buried in national cemeteries, where the headstones are uniformly white with identical style identification, row upon row, but that nearly half of those are unidentified!

## A World's Fair Phenomenon

Americans have never tired of studying the Civil War, looking at photos and paintings of it and trying perhaps to understand how such an internal struggle could take place within their own country, how 600,000 Americans could be casualties of a war between brothers. The country east of the Mississippi was still small, and the colonies had only officially been the United States, as Lincoln said, for "four score and seven years." Perhaps by looking in the eyes of that conflict, at the death and destruction, we can prevent such things from ever happening again.

Over the years, many world's fairs included special Civil War attractions. In Seattle, at the Alaska-Yukon Pacific Exposition in 1909, the "Pay Streak" midway featured a reenactment of the battle between the *Monitor* and the *Merrimac*.

During what was possibly our country's most historic world's fair, the 1893 World's Columbian Exposition in Chicago, a massive "cyclorama," or "picture in the round," of the Battle of Gettysburg was exhibited in the city, not actually on the fairgrounds.

Also displayed at the Columbian Exposition was French artist Paul Philippoteaux's painting of the Gettysburg tableaux, which he did some 20 years after the battle. After the exposition, the painting was taken on a national tour and last shown back in Chicago at the 1933 Century of Progress world's fair. It then vanished. Fortunately, Philippoteaux painted a second one, which has been on display at Gettysburg and was recently given a $9 million restoration.

The missing original was found in storage in 1965, coincidentally, the 100th anniversary of the end of the war. It was appraised at $2.5 million some years ago and no doubt would be worth many times that amount today. If you have the pocket change—and room for the 376-foot-wide, six-ton painting—it is currently rolled up in 14 very large storage cylinders.

## April 14, 1865

President Abraham Lincoln is shot by John Wilkes Booth.

## April 15, 1865

Lincoln dies.

### John Wilkes Booth, Actor and Assassin

John Wilkes Booth was part of a very prominent acting family, and he was almost maniacal in his hatred of Lincoln, the Union and the freeing of slaves. He hatched a plan to kidnap Lincoln and several members of his cabinet, but when that scheme became too cumbersome, he decided to assassinate the president instead.

On April 14, 1865, Lincoln's personal guards were away, and the president was in his private box watching a play at Washington's Ford Theater. Booth waited until the guards left the entrance to Lincoln's box, then walked in and shot the president directly in the back of the head with a pistol.

Lincoln was essentially dead at that moment, though he spent the night in a coma before passing away the following morning. What Booth accomplished was to take away the leader who was about to start rebuilding the South, making Lincoln a martyr in the eyes of all who believed in his ability to restore the country to its former strength.

It took more than a week for U.S. troops to locate Booth and put him to death, and the country moved swiftly to capture, try and execute Booth's conspirators.

In some very ironic and coincidental twists of fate, Lincoln's son, Robert Todd, had his life intertwined with other presidential assassinations and with the Booth family. Some months before Abraham Lincoln's assassination, Booth's brother, Edwin, a renowned actor himself, happened to be on the same crowded train platform as Robert. The youngster slipped and was trapped between the train and the platform when someone reached out and pulled him to safety. His rescuer was Edwin Booth, whom Robert immediately recognized because of his fame as an actor! Later, as an adult, Robert was visiting the 1901 Pan American World's Fair in Buffalo, New York, at the invitation of President McKinley, who was assassinated on the grounds. And when President Garfield was assassinated in 1881 in Washington, DC, Robert was near him and an eyewitness to the event.

## The First Woman Executed in the U.S.

Booth's plots to kidnap aside, he was not satisfied with killing only the president. He had conspirators attempting to assassinate Vice President Johnson and Secretary of State Seward, as well. He fully believed that even though General Lee had surrendered and the South was in shambles, the war was not over.

There was no question that public opinion, and political opinion for that matter, clamored for swift action and executions of Booth and his accomplices. Mary Surratt was convicted despite her continuing pleas that she had never seen any other conspirators and was simply going to collect rent money at her boarding house, not meeting anyone to finalize plans to kill Lincoln. However, witnesses and conspirators had her playing an integral role in the planning of Lincoln's assassination, enough to earn her the death penalty.

Many were sure her sentence would be commuted to life imprisonment, since no woman had ever been executed in the U.S. She and other conspirators were kept heavily shackled in irons on a warship as their prison from the time of their capture until they were hanged. The military court recommended to President Johnson that the sentence be changed to life in prison. He ignored the request and claimed that he had never seen the document requesting the change, despite the fact that the tribunal head who wrote to him said he had discussed it with the president. It was just one of many instances of confusion and contradiction that surrounded Johnson as president.

Surratt was hooded while in prison to keep her from attempting suicide, as well as for her hanging and burial afterward. It was clear that her neck was broken immediately as she was hanged, while two of her co-conspirators could be seen struggling for up to five minutes as they slowly choked to death.

After Surratt's hanging, part of the rope and locks of her hair were sold as souvenirs.

## Camp and Outpost Duty for Infantry

In camp, the best water will be pointed out before the men are dismissed, and the necessary directions for opening communications, etc., given. All parties sent out of camp to bathe, wash, or for any other purposed, must be under charge of a properly authorized officer.

The Lincoln family seemed cursed with tragedy, but so many other families could cite similar troubles—or worse—during the Civil War.

Mary Todd Lincoln suffered terrible headaches during her stay in the White House, which today would likely be diagnosed as either stress or tension headaches, or possibly migraines. She also was subject to fits of anger, and after her husband's death, to bouts of not just anger, but also confusion and disorientation. Scholars believe she was bipolar.

Lincoln was said to suffer bouts of melancholy, which would be considered clinical depression in today's medical diagnoses.

Besides the monumental stress of leading the nation at war, the Lincolns were parents to four boys. Sadly, only one, their firstborn, lived to adulthood. Robert Todd Lincoln was born in 1843, when Lincoln was 34. He had three children and lived to the age of 82. Middle sons Edward and Willie died very young, and the youngest, Tad, outlived his father, but died at age 18 in 1871. The last direct descendent of Abraham Lincoln, Robert's grandson Todd Lincoln Beckwith, died in 1985, ending the Lincoln family line.

## Lincoln's Funeral Train

Abraham Lincoln's body was embalmed by the same man who embalmed his son Tad, and who was reportedly hired for the task by Mrs. Lincoln after she recalled the fine job he had done on the body of Colonel E.E. Elsworth, considered the first Civil War casualty. Elsworth, who became a folk hero of the war, was shot while removing a Confederate flag he discovered on a building in Alexandria, Virginia, in May 1861.

Lincoln's special funeral train left Washington for the meandering ride home to Springfield, Illinois. Along the way, there were public viewings and memorial services. Souvenir cards, ribbons and other items remain very sought-after and expensive remembrances even today. The train made stops in

Baltimore, Maryland; Harrisburg and Philadelphia, Pennsylvania; New York City, Albany and Buffalo, New York; Cleveland and Columbus, Ohio; Indianapolis and Michigan City, Indiana; Chicago and, finally, Springfield, Illinois. People came out at every stop, and even between them, to catch at least a glimpse of Lincoln's train, if not of the fallen president's body.

## Camp and Outpost Duty for Infantry

The proper formation of a dress parade adds much to its effectiveness, simplicity, and precision.

## A Final Tally from the Union Surgeon General

Nine years after the war, the Adjutant General and the Surgeon General combined to issue a report that they felt represented the *final* numbers—statistics about enlistment, injuries and deaths—their departments could compile after nearly a decade of post–Civil War research:

☞ The United States government cited "2,073,111 enlisted and 178,895 colored soldiers" serving in the Union army—a total of 2,252,006 enlisted men.

☞ A total of 285,545 enlisted men were discharged for some type of disability—12.7 percent of all enlisted men in the Union army.

☞ Some of the more significant causes for discharge and the total number of men released for each were:

| | |
|---|---|
| Consumption | 20,403 |
| Dysentery | 17,389 |
| Debility | 14,500 |
| Rheumatism | 11,779 |
| Heart disease | 10,636 |

The final report also noted that the greatest cause of death was dysentery, but we have found contradictory numbers within the federal reports, which cite 149,043 and also 186,216 dying from the disease. Further research would, no doubt, eventually solve that contradiction.

The same report also noted the total figure for white soldiers, probably enlisted men as per the previous breakdown, who died during the war as 217,124—10.5 percent of all white enlisted men. The 33,380 deaths of black soldiers, on the other hand, represents a whopping 18.7 percent of all black enlisted men.

| | |
|---|---|
| Deaths of white soldiers | 217,124 |
| Deaths of black soldiers | 33,380 |

## Between Survival and the Rest of Their Lives

When Union soldiers were discharged from the service because of illness, injury or in a prisoner-of-war trade with the Confederates, their first destination was usually a Sanitary Commission house, a hotel or a hospital.

The Sanitary Commission, which had blossomed into tens of thousands of volunteers all over the North, used donated funds to establish facilities to help usher soldiers back into civilian life. Heading the Commission was Frederick Law Olmsted, one of the foremost landscape architects in the country. Among his works are New York's Central Park and Chicago's World's Columbian Exposition of 1893, as well as

### Camp and Outpost Duty for Infantry

The officer of the day is charged with the order and cleanliness of the camp. He has the calls beaten by the drummer of the guard.

dozens of parks and facilities considered the finest in each of the American cities in which he designed them.

The Sanitary Commission facilities in Washington, DC, at the height of the war, for example, were in a constant state of expansion to handle all the soldiers coming through that city on their way home. The organization provided the tangibles—clothing, medical care, food, toiletries, books, writing material (items that they provided to troops in the field, as well)—but, more importantly, the intangibles such as doctors to talk with, staff to help with the return home, a warm bed in which to relax and a way to try to rid themselves of the horrors they had just experienced. Although recuperation was recognized to be both physical and emotional, there were no counselors or psychiatrists, and the terminology to describe mental illnesses such as post-traumatic stress disorder didn't yet exist. But the care of the soldiers went far beyond their physical wounds.

"Before these returned prisoners left us for their homes," Frederick N. Knapp, special relief agent and head of the facility in the nation's capital said, "each one was provided with whatever undergarments he needed, and all who desire them, with blankets." It seemed an odd combination, when you would expect to see a list including shirts, shoes, pants, toothbrushes and so on.

> ## December 6, 1865
> The 13th Amendment is ratified.

## Post-war Pensions

The United States government handed out large numbers of veterans' checks after the Civil War ended, recognizing not just military service, but also additional hardships that soldiers suffered. Considering the massive number of non-fatal casualties, the Union had hundreds of thousands of seriously disabled veterans returning home to farms and factories where they could no longer work.

Soldiers, as well as sailors and marines, who suffered various disabilities were given additional federal pensions. And considering the vast numbers involved, the government moved much more quickly than one would imagine. Without computers, phones and databases of Social Security numbers, dog tags or serial numbers, soldiers waited up to a year or more for their claims to be processed. But that was because of the sheer volume. The process was quickly smoothed out, veterans filled out forms with their unit number, the date they were sworn in and discharged, and details of their injury. Considering the magnitude of the task at hand, it was amazing what was accomplished, including both building hospitals and creating comprehensive systems to handle injured veterans.

Photos of crippled soldiers standing outside clapboard buildings waiting in line after the war paint a grim picture, but new technology grew out of the aftermath of the war just as it did during the conflict. The development of prosthetics improved dramatically, and medical science made huge strides. Military pensions couldn't bring back an eye or a limb, but considering the low wages of the time, the extra money could replace lost income.

## Camp and Outpost Duty for Infantry

Each time a man goes on duty as a sentry, he must have the same post that he had the first time—the most intelligent, trusty, and experienced soldiers being chosen for the most difficult and important posts.

# What's It Worth?

Beginning immediately after the war, disability pensions were as follows:

| Injury | Compensation |
| --- | --- |
| Loss of just one foot or just one hand | $15* |
| Incapacitated, unable to perform manual labor | $20 |
| Loss of both feet | $20* |
| Loss of one hand *and* one foot | $20* |
| Incapacitated, requiring the assistance of another person | $25 |
| Loss of sight in both eyes | $25* |
| Loss of both hands | $25* |

Nine years later, in 1874, the pensions were raised for all those disabilities marked with an asterisk (*) to $50.

When abolitionist Senator Charles M. Sumner passed away the decade after the war, one of the executors of his will was poet Henry W. Longfellow.

## Still No Rest

In December 1865, the United States Naval Asylum in Philadelphia advertised for a contractor interested in immediate work—to exhume all the bodies of the naval veterans in the "old" cemetery of that institution so that they could be re-interred at the United States Naval Cemetery at Mount Moriah in Philadelphia, Pennsylvania. It was not clear if a single contract would cover both exhumation and reburial, or if separate contracts would be awarded.

# WHO ARE THE COLLECTORS?

A Confederate postage stamp, genuine and used during the war

## Something for Everyone

Few topics are as collectible as the Civil War, and there are literally millions of individuals in the United States with more than a passing interest in the period. Generally, the less involved and less sophisticated the collector, the broader the scope of collecting; one contradiction to this general rule is if the new collector was introduced to the hobby with an immediate, very narrow purpose, such as collecting only those items pertaining to Great-great-great-great-uncle Phineas' South Carolina regiment, or perhaps a seamstress is asked to sew uniforms for reenactors, in which case the next step might be very serious collecting of everything to do with original uniforms and women's clothing of the Civil War period.

As a collector learns more, collects more and thus spends more, he or she begins filling in that basic knowledge with expertise in more specialized areas. For example, there are books pertaining to uniforms and clothing worn during the

Civil War, and almost every regiment has been the subject of a modern book or a rare, old volume. You might find a comprehensive new book on a well-known or famous regiment for $19.95, a regimental history published in 1867 might cost $500 or a reprint of that title issued, say, in 1910 for a reunion might cost only $100.

Some people collect *only* items that pertain to a relative, a relative's unit or their home state. Many, of course, collect only Union or only Confederate, and then there are those who collect Abraham Lincoln or weapons exclusively.

As far-reaching and important as the Civil War was, likewise, its effect on collectors has been immense. All this is terribly superficial, but new collectors often—*very often*—ask "How much will I need to spend?" Some collectors are on a different side of the fence. These are the ones who routinely pay $500, $1000 or even $10,000 per item. At the same time, a much larger number of collectors might have an annual budget of only a few thousand dollars.

There are serious collectors who may attend many collector shows each year, read appropriate publications and spend hours each week online—yet spend perhaps no more than $600 to $800 and purchase just a handful of items. Expenditures have never been a useful gauge for a collector's annual budget of time.

## Camp and Outpost Duty for Infantry

All deserters from the enemy, and other persons coming within our lines, will be taken at once to the provost marshal of the nearest division, who will examine them in presence of the division commander, or an officer of his staff designated for the purpose, and communicate the result and the information obtained to the provost marshal.

# GETTING STARTED

## Deciding What to Collect

A sewing kit that folded or rolled up and held needles,
buttons, thread and fabric patches

If you are interested in the Civil War and have collected
other types of items in the past, that is by far the best way
to introduce yourself to the hobby. For example, one of the
oldest hobbies worldwide is coin collecting, and the Civil
War spawned many new areas for numismatists and collectors of related items. Civil War tokens, probably not known

to many non-collectors, were produced only during part of the war, yet estimates are that 50 million were struck in some 10,000 different designs. Tokens are split into "patriotics" and "store cards." Both may have a patriotic obverse—showing Washington, Lincoln or crossed flags, for example—but the patriotics will have a related theme on the reverse, whereas store cards will advertise a business—a market, bookstore, tavern, hat store, baker, undertaker or almost any business you could imagine. There are many good-quality references in the marketplace that will let you know what a given token may sell for depending on its condition and rarity. With modest rarity and condition expectations, tokens might cost from $15 to $50 each, with 90 percent of them at the low end of the price spectrum. But for rare, high-grade specimens—for example, those with fewer than 10 tokens known to exist—you may find yourself spending from $100 to $1000 each time you find one you "need."

If you are especially interested in weapons, be forewarned that the hobby gets pricey—you can easily spend thousands of dollars to purchase a quality Colt revolver or a Springfield rifle without getting near the "rare" weapons category. A better tactic might be to learn about the weapons and make it a long-term project to search for an item you can afford. If you are disciplined, devote some effort to learning about the subject and spend some time window-shopping, you will build

## Camp and Outpost Duty for Infantry

Field officer of the day should see that the butchers of the brigade or regiments dig proper trenches for the reception of all refuse matter, that it is buried, and the vicinity made and kept wholesome.

expertise very quickly. In the meantime, you can purchase inexpensive (relatively speaking) complementary items, from various caliber bullets to cartridge boxes to original manuals and army documents.

Collecting by geographic area or regiment can be much easier and much less expensive, though some items you find may be rare and will be priced accordingly.

Union army uniform buttons

## Topics and Areas of Interest

The Civil War encompasses not just a broad spectrum of American history, but hundreds, even thousands, of narrower-scope topics. A serious collector or hobbyist of the Civil War might easily be more or less expert in numerous subject areas, and he or she might then collect specifically from the Civil War or collect similar objects from other wars, countries or eras. Many simply collect "the Civil War" at the beginning, and then begin to develop specialties over time as their interests and knowledge grow more sophisticated.

## Camp and Outpost Duty for Infantry

The quarter-master will keep a statistical record, showing, in perfect and minute detail, the working of his train; the number of horses to each wagon; the amount in kind and weight of forage given to each horse; the weight of the horses or mules; the weight of the wagon, harness and driver; the number of miles traveled each day; the weight of the load, etc.

Here are some areas of specialization:

☛ **Individual weapons:** rifles, bayonets, pistols, bullets, swords, boot pistols, knives

☛ **Non-individual weapons:** howitzers, cannons, fixed guns, navy guns, torpedoes (and yes, there are collectors who purchase these massive weapons!)

☛ **Personal military accoutrements:** uniforms and items from uniforms, coats, hats, insignia, haversacks, cartridge boxes, percussion cap containers, blankets, buttons

☛ **Camp needs:** razors, toothbrushes, eyeglasses, sewing kits (called "housewives"), inkwells, fountain pens, pencils, utensils, coffee pots, dishes, diaries, letters, entertainment items such as dominoes, dice, cards or carvings

☛ **Tobacciana:** tobacco tins and labels, sealed tins and packets of tobacco, carved pipes

☛ **Books and literature:** historical, modern, periodicals, original documents, diaries, letters (these may be categorized by topic or individual and the type of letter, such as those written between couples or those with military content or of geographical interest)

☛ **Modern entertainment about the Civil War:** items related to films, television or books about the war, either fiction or nonfiction

☛ **On the home front:** women's and children's clothing and accessories, cooking- or farming-related items, household objects, photographs

☛ **Musical instruments:** regimental bugles and drums, marching band items, soldiers' personal Jew's harps, harmonicas and so on

☛ **Autographs:** these can range from the signatures of any-one involved with the Civil War to only those of soldiers in a certain unit, or perhaps just generals or politicians (The most expensive? Abraham Lincoln and Robert E. Lee, always in demand, plus those who died without signing much, such as Stonewall Jackson or the infa-mous Custer)

☛ **Coins and stamps:** actual period coins and currency, trade tokens, sutler tokens and chits, dog tags, military medals, publicly awarded medals, Union and Confederate stamps, postal indicia, patriotic envelopes, private- and government-issued currency, stocks or bonds, modern commemorative medals and stamps

☛ **Lincolniana:** one of the largest categories of Civil War collecting that essentially encompasses everything listed here plus almost anything related to Lincoln, from his autograph to mourning paraphernalia

☛ **Modern reproductions and topics:** clothing, toys, movie memorabilia and so on; beware, there are myriad facsimiles and there are always people anxious to offer them as genuine items.

## Camp and Outpost Duty for Infantry

In case of desertion, the position of the guard is to be changed, the officer made acquainted with the fact, increased vigilance used, and the desertion immediately reported, and the countersign and signals changed by proper authority.

# Educating Yourself

Commit time to education, and as you do so, consider learning from the 1860s, not just the present. Build an inexpensive contemporary library—start looking in used bookstores for early references, and you will likely find a passion developing for not just the Civil War, but also for some specific aspect of it. The best time to launch your collecting is when you have begun to understand life during that period in the country's history.

If you are already a bona fide collector, expand your area of interest to include the Civil War. Even if you think your hobby doesn't translate well to the period, you may be surprised. For example, if you collect aviation-related items, you could look into things pertaining to early spy balloons. If you love railroading, there was no bigger period of excitement in the country's railroading than the 1860s. Collecting memorabilia of the 20th century could be supplemented by expanding your interest to include Civil War railroads.

Take a trip online through eBay or browse antique malls and see where your searches lead you. The more you know about your subject from the beginning, the less often you will have to utter the collector's lament: "If I only knew what it was worth at the time…" Besides, there's nothing like going to a coin show and discovering that all your reading has paid off as you discover a scarce or even rare Civil War token or dog tag just knocking around in a dealer's "bargain box" marked "Your Choice—$1 Each!"

## Camp and Outpost Duty for Infantry

Regimental surgeons will be held responsible that the hospital service in their regiments is kept constantly effective, and in readiness for any emergency. No remissions in this respect will be tolerated or overlooked.

# AVOID GETTING YOUR POCKET PICKED

## Buyer Beware

If you have lived on the planet for a long time or have been collecting for a number of years, you have likely learned quite painfully that there are deceitful people, downright liars and shady sellers who can smile through a dishonest transaction as easily as taking a breath.

The key is to pay attention *and* to educate yourself. The best investment you can make is to create a personal library—it can grow as large as you want it to—about the Civil War and the areas in which you are collecting. Unfortunately, all the pretty books on store shelves are not necessarily good. Take the time to purchase references that you know are respected by bookstore people (they hear complaints when a book is bad) and fellow collectors. We're not talking about buying collectible vintage or rare books, not yet—those can come later, when you want to invest in books written and/or published during or immediately after the war.

You will also want to know how much things are worth, and most price guides in *every* hobby area overstate value. Consider joining a local Civil War Roundtable—there are hundreds, maybe more than a 1000, in communities throughout the U.S. They meet monthly or quarterly to discuss aspects of the Civil War, historical analysis and collecting, too.

For every bit of information you receive, you will hear something contradictory, but that's the way of collecting in this and so many other fields. You must be patient and remember that the one person on whom you can rely to be honest and educated is *yourself.*

## Camp and Outpost Duty for Infantry

In advancing into a portion of the country which has not been thoroughly and recently reconnoitered, too much caution can not be observed to guard against surprise and ambuscade.

# OTHER COLLECTIBLES

## Was There a Mickey Mantle in the CW?

In the early 1960s, with baseball card collecting an unbelievably popular craze, can you imagine companies getting rich, a nickel at a time?

Baseball card collectors, back then with an average age of eight to 11 years old, made the Topps Company an unprecedented success. And with the 1961–1965 Civil War centennial underway, do you think a card manufacturer already famous for Planes, Elvis, Tarzan, Spacemen and Zorro, among others, would skip the Civil War?

The cards were called "Civil War News" and were issued with that wonderful smelly slab of pink gum, made from sugar and covered with some mysterious powder, accompanied by a terrific insert in each pack—a piece of genuine facsimile Confederate currency, which looked pretty darned real. We're sure that more than a couple of pieces of that currency found their way into antique stores to be sold as the real thing.

The cards were issued in the famous "wax packs," sealed with hot wax, at a nickel per pack, as well as "cello packs" in see-through cello wrap, similarly sealed and with the currency showing in different denominations per pack. There were also "rack packs," consisting of three individual cello packs wrapped together as a 15-cent, three-pack special.

### Camp and Outpost Duty for Infantry

The commanding officer of the regiment will make frequent inspections of the kitchen and messes. These duties are of the utmost importance—not to be neglected.

The best thing about these very cool color cards? You can still find them today at card stores and on eBay, and occasionally an unopened pack will show up, too, for all of you just dying to go back in time to when you wore a Davy Crockett coonskin cap, had a rubber-banded stack of baseball cards in one pocket, with those non-sports cards like Civil War News in a different rubber band—and your duplicates clothes-pinned to your spokes on that balloon-tired bike. A nickel! Just think for a minute what a dollar could buy at the local corner grocery back then…

## Little-Known Confederate Money

When Southern currency shrunk to the point of having virtually no value as the war went on, the Confederates—in secret—decided to create their own small change. Whether it was a statement of their outlook or just a fanciful task to make themselves feel like a *real* penniless country, the Confederate States of America (CSA) created both one-cent coins and half-dollars. When a suit of clothes cost nearly $3000 (in nearly worthless Confederate currency), a shiny penny might buy a button—or, better still, be substituted for one.

The Confederate government retained Robert Lovett Jr. of Philadelphia to create coining dies, but after doing so, he panicked and hid them because he feared imprisonment in the North. It's unclear if 12 or 14 original cent pieces were struck, but today they're highly valued as collector's items, as are later restrikes. But in 1865, it might have taken 10 times more pennies than were made to buy a piece of "penny" candy.

The CSA struck four test half-dollars, but they were never put into circulation or minted in any additional quantity. However, thanks to the ever-present scrutiny of vigilant collectors—rather than historians—the coins eventually found their way into the public eye. One was sold at auction in 2003—for $632,500. Now, that was inflation, but it was paid for with United States, not Confederate, funds.

The morale? Don't print millions of pieces of worthless currency when you can *make* millions of dollars by minting just one or two of something that will become collectible.

## Camp and Outpost Duty for Infantry

When an army is on the march, if it is desired to protect the property of the inhabitants, the provost detail from each regiment, or a portion of it, should march on its flank, and prevent soldiers from entering any premises.

## Never Forgot

In 1866, the Grand Army of the Republic (GAR) was formed as a fraternal organization for the veterans of the Union forces in the Civil War. The counterpart in the South was the Sons of the Confederacy. There were also auxiliaries for wives and sons and daughters.

The organizations held reunions from coast to coast and well into the 20th century…until there weren't very many left to attend such events. The GAR carried immense clout in the 19th century; if you were running for office, it was like having the Teamsters behind you.

Today, with the oldest living vets of the war having been dead for 50 years or so, one might think these organizations have disappeared. But reenactors today are, for the most part, the great-great-grandchildren of those soldiers, sailors and marines.

And if you collect Civil War memorabilia, the medals, badges, ribbons, canteens, pipes, belts, pins and more issued by these organizations are treasures. The universal GAR badge, authorized by Congress, with a bronze star and a ribbon, can be acquired for as little as $20. A commander's ribbon might fetch $1000 if it's rare, and like any other collectible, when there are thousands of collectors, you know there must be thousands of sellers—and all the items that one could want to own. People collect the badges by date, by "encampment" (the national and local annual events and gatherings), by unit and even by auxiliary.

## When There's No Paper, Just Print on the Walls

That wasn't exactly the case, but close. There were so many shortages in the South that it's difficult to keep track of the myriad hardships suffered by residents. With most of the factories located in the North, the South ran out of necessities quickly. News was of vital interest, but newspapers in the South found themselves having to curtail the number of copies printed. At one point, in Mississippi, paper was simply no longer available, so some papers took to issuing their news printed on the back of ornate wallpaper!

The wallpaper was cut to standard newspaper size, and single sheets, one sided, were issued to subscribers. The novelty of this, and the rarity of just a handful surviving, made them expensive collectibles even shortly after the war. Entrepreneurs— or hustlers—began reprinting war-date wallpaper newspapers and selling them to Northerners first as souvenirs, then as rare originals. As with any such counterfeits, minor differences in a date or a line break are the only ways to differentiate the originals from the fakes. Today, the facsimiles printed a year or two after the war still can command prices of several hundred dollars, whereas the originals continue to increase in value and could easily bring $3000 to $6000 in the collector marketplace.

## Forging Lincoln's Signature

Autograph collecting was very popular, even in the Civil War era, and grew more popular in later years. Abraham Lincoln was gracious about signing autographs for those who mailed him requests (remember, it wasn't done on a moment's notice on the street when there were no ballpoint pens or Sharpies; the signer needed a fountain pen and inkwell), and as noted in the section about Sanitary Fairs, the president donated signed documents to be auctioned at fairs to raise money for the war effort.

After Lincoln's death, the popularity of his signature sky-rocketed, and just like today, the vultures descended on the collectibles market. There were master forgers who created and sold Lincoln's autograph with slight variations in dates and forms. Today, many of those forgeries remain, and some are of such high quality that even the best 21st-century experts cannot tell an 1860s forgery from the real thing. Collectors are always cautioned to know the seller and his or her credentials before purchasing anything. The unscrupulous sellers in the Americana and autograph fields, just like those who have haunted the coin, stamp and sports markets for decades, come in all shapes, suits and personalities!

### Camp and Outpost Duty for Infantry

The sentinels should be instructed to observe carefully the nature of the ground, and to select such places of protection for themselves as their posts will afford.

# WHATEVER YOUR PLEASURE TO SEE THE CIVIL WAR

## Telling the Story

Whatever your pleasure today, there never has been a paucity of opportunities for viewing or reading all about the Civil War of 150 year ago. From the day the war erupted at Fort Sumter, there were newspaper accounts available, more so in the North, but also in the South.

After the war, book upon book erupted onto the scene. They were published abroad as well as in the United States. There were regimental histories—first-person accounts of the glory of the war by the men who did the fighting. There were also soldiers' diaries, some of which became part of family histories. Bibles had papers inserted in them, and tens of thousands of families had collections of letters from sons and other male relatives who went off to war. Too many widows had stacks of letters and little else by which they could remember their husbands.

### Camp and Outpost Duty for Infantry

Passes to citizens within the lines, and for purposes of trade, may be granted by the provost marshals, general and local, who will be guided strictly by the instructions heretofore given by headquarters upon the subject.

## From Story to History

By the late 19th century, hundreds upon hundreds of campfire tales, stories of battles, accounts of suffering in prisoner-of-war camps and innumerable new editions of regimental histories and tales of the war were all published as books written for veterans and for those born in the decades that had passed since the war ended. While much of the literature was educational, a good deal of it martyred the country's losses, none with more fervor and devotion than what was written about Abraham Lincoln. Stage plays told the story of war and our country's loss of innocence.

By the time the 20th century dawned, the feeling that the Civil War was a story "about us" had faded and become the story of "our history."

## Camp and Outpost Duty for Infantry

The field-officer of the day will visit the reserves, supports, and pickets soon after they are posted, and at least once during the night. He will see that they are in proper positions, and connect through the whole line of his brigade.

# ON THE SILVER SCREEN

*A comprehensive listing and reviews of films about the Civil War is outside the scope of this book, but what follows is a selection of some of the better examples of the genre. Myriad films have had some portion of their content set in the Civil War or handled as part of serious issues in U.S. history, from slavery to prejudice.*

## Gone With the Wind

From the time of the earliest motion pictures—the first silent movies—there were films about the Civil War. And then, in 1939, along came the most famous of all Civil War movies, entertaining audiences with its melodramatic tenor and ushering in the era of color in films.

Based on the novel by Margaret Mitchell, *Gone With the Wind* took the world by storm. Suave Clark Gable and relatively unknown (in the U.S.) actress Vivien Leigh starred in David O. Selznick's epic film. The novel was a Pulitzer Prize winner, and the book sold a million copies in roughly six months. The film, twice the length of a typical movie, was 16 minutes short of *four* hours. For the longest time, it was considered the consummate Civil War film. In fact, some criticized Mitchell's book because it followed the war quite chronologically, and the passion and relationships were overlaid, and sometimes overwhelmed by, the strong historical background.

Today, for someone looking for Civil War entertainment, whether fiction or nonfiction, *Gone With the Wind* stands head and shoulders above most other movies. It is one of the 100 best films of all time, first by many accounts, and, based on tickets sold (rather than revenue, which loses perspective over time), it is the best-selling film of all time, as well.

# The Birth of a Nation

Students of the Civil War or film aficionados should seek out the ultimate silent movie, *The Birth of a Nation*, directed by D.W. Griffith, which was first shown almost a century ago in 1915. Although its portrayal of the period is somewhat controversial, it holds a place of honor in film history, and, despite its age, perspective and lack of today's Hollywood magic, the movie can still be valuable to both film buffs and Civil War buffs alike.

## The Red Badge of Courage

The 1951 film *The Red Badge of Courage* was directed by John Huston, with World War II hero Audie Murphy interestingly cast in the lead. Based on the book written by Stephen Crane and published in 1895, it tells the story of a young Union soldier struggling to overcome fear and finding courage in the heat of battle during the Civil War. However, the film was more of a critical than a box office success.

## Camp and Outpost Duty for Infantry

No man should be chosen for provost guard duty who cannot read and write. As it is highly important that all attempts at forgeries in passes, safeguards, should be immediately detected. Any neglect in this respect might sacrifice an army.

# Star Power

Hollywood used the Civil War in vehicles for many stars, though not all of them were serious actors, all the films not award winners and not are all household names for the current generation of moviegoers. Here's a list of actors and the Civil War films in which they appeared:

| | |
|---|---|
| John Wayne | *The Horse Soldiers* (1959) |
| Charlton Heston | *Three Violent People* (1956) |
| | *Major Dundee* (1965) |
| William Holden | *The Man from Colorado* (1948) |
| | *Escape from Fort Bravo* (1953) |
| Clint Eastwood | *The Beguiled* (1971) |
| Gary Cooper | *Only the Brave* (1930) |
| | *Springfield Rifle* (1952) |
| Red Skelton | *Whistling in Dixie* (1942) |
| | *A Southern Yankee* (1948) |
| James Stewart | *Of Human Hearts* (1938) |
| | *Shenandoah* (1965) |

## Camp and Outpost Duty for Infantry

Men should never be allowed to void their excrement elsewhere than in the regular established sinks. In well-regulated camps the sinks are visited daily by a police part, a layer of earth thrown in, and lime and other disinfecting agents employed to prevent them from becoming offensive and unhealthy.

# Looking for Glory

Numerous other films of the last 25 or 30 years have been less overwhelming as events, but still rate highly as "entertainment" for Civil War fans. Many of these have been more high drama and perhaps less history, but were set in the proper time and place, nevertheless.

One of this era's major award-winning films was well deserving of the honor and historically sound. The 1989 film *Glory* told the story of the first black regiment to be thrust into battle during the Civil War, the Massachusetts 54th.

The film featured Matthew Broderick in a role more powerful than many of his others, playing the part of Robert
Gould Shaw, the white officer who led the 54th and died
with them. Morgan Freeman and Denzel Washington gave
their typically outstanding performances, and Washington
won an Oscar for Best Supporting Actor for his role.

# Cold Mountain

The most recent "outstanding" Civil War movie on most
reviewers' lists is the 2003 *Cold Mountain*, which had a slew
of top actors and actresses in the cast, including Jude Law,
Nicole Kidman, Renee Zellweger (who won an Oscar for her
supporting role), Natalie Portman and Donald Sutherland.
Based on Charles Frazier's best-selling novel of the same
name, it tells the story of a Confederate deserter trying to
make his way home to the woman he loves and also high-
lights the hardships of those living in the South.

Interest in the Civil War has been strong in the 150 years
since it was fought, but every time an author or filmmaker
stirs our consciousness (and our conscience!), book sales,
National Park visits, movie sales and other measures of
interest in our bloodiest war of all time skyrocket.

## Camp and Outpost Duty for Infantry

Every favorable position must be seized by the commander to make a stand against the pursuers with his
infantry; charge their advanced lines with his cavalry,
and bring his artillery into battery; always bearing in
mind that it may at any moment be possible, by energetic action and judicious management to entirely
check the pursuit, or even to turn defeat into victory.

# ON THE SMALL SCREEN

*In the 20th century, "made for TV" movies and "mini-series" became crossover events that offered elements of both television and film, and however good or bad the productions were, audiences never seemed to lose their exuberance for the topic of the Civil War. Some of the finest television specials and serializations featuring the Civil War were made in the 1970s and '80s, and most have never been seen by younger generations.*

## Roots

The 1977 epic, *Roots*, and its sequel, *Roots: The Next Generations*, followed the lives of one family, from the capture of a young African in the 18th century through his horrifying ride to America in the hold of a slave ship, to a plantation, and then to the Civil War and beyond. Author Alex Haley told the story of his own family, which he traced from that first adolescent African who was captured— Haley's great-great-great-great-grandfather—through a total of seven generations between Haley and "the African" Kunta Kinte. Haley won a Pulitzer Prize for the book, while the 10-hour television production won nine Emmy Awards. Certainly the massive book and the lengthy mini-series both belong on Civil War lists. This book-TV special, however, is the story of slavery, not *just* the story of the war. It spawned a huge interest in genealogy and also in the development of other mini-series "events" on television.

Two other the outstanding Civil War mini-series were the 1982 *The Blue and the Gray* and the 1985 *North and South*.

## Educating the Public

Ken Burns' documentary, *The Civil War*, aired on PBS in 1990, six years after he began research to tell the complete story of the war in the words of those who fought and lived and died, combined with 16,000 archival photographs that Burns studied and used in the production. The response to the series was overwhelming, and, like many other productions noted here, the perception and level of knowledge of the public changed dramatically with the presentation of the Civil War in films, documentaries and books.

### Camp and Outpost Duty for Infantry

The contents of each and every wagon in the train should be known to all officers in charge or connected therewith.

## In the Zone

How many television shows have presented *five* episodes devoted to the Civil War? These five were all from the eerie, sci-fi-like weekly series of the early 1960s, *The Twilight Zone*. Rod Serling was a master of television and imagination, and had he not passed away at only 50 years of age, more cinematic masterpieces—perhaps revolving around the Civil War—would have been ours to enjoy.

- ☞ **Long Live Walter Jameson (1960):** A college professor has been living for eternity, and his secret is revealed for the first time when his fiancée's father recognizes him in a photo of Union officers taken a century earlier.

- ☞ **Back There (1961):** This episode takes place in a private club in the present, until a gentleman walks out the door and into history, following a discussion about whether one could change history or not.

☛ **The Passersby (1961):** A woman watches a seemingly endless trail of exhausted and wounded Civil War soldiers pass by her home, refusing to believe that her husband was killed. She finally understands the meaning of the scene when the last man on the road is Abraham Lincoln.

☛ **Still Valley (1961):** A Confederate soldier has a choice, victory (through a pact with the devil) or to let the war end with a Southern defeat.

☛ **An Occurrence at Owl Creek Bridge (1964):** This is the only episode of the series that was written outside the production company. It was originally a French film based on an 1895 short story about a Civil War spy who may or may not have escaped his hanging from the Owl Creek Bridge.

## Camp and Outpost Duty for Infantry

The duties of regimental officers of the day and guard, if properly performed, are calculated to increase the efficiency, drill, and reliability of a regiment under more serious circumstances, as on picket and other duties, and the battlefield, where the principles of correct deportment, vigilance, and soldierly respect will bear fruit in a like observation when its effect will influence the fate of an army in battle.

## Camp and Outpost Duty for Infantry

The moment a regiment arrives at camp, men found without a pass, visiting barns, out-houses, or private dwellings, foraging, going from one brigade to another or wandering anywhere out of their camp, will be arrested and punished; and if on the march, made to march in disgrace at the rear.

## Civil War TV Quiz: For Baby Boomers Only

What television series with a Civil War connection aired from 1959 to 1961? Can you name the show, the Civil War connection and the actor who starred in the series? Bonus points if you know who sang the theme song.

For some of us—probably 98 percent of whom were boys about 10 years old—*this* was real historical stuff.

Of course, the answer is *The Rebel*, set in the West just after the Civil War, and starring the late Nick Adams as Johnny Yuma, a young ex-Rebel soldier with a chip on his shoulder who was always looking to do a good deed—an odd combination in the Old West.

Remember the song? "Johnny Yu-maaw, was a rebel, he roamed through the West, and Johnny Yu-maaw, he wan-der-ed alone." The singer? Who else could have done as fine a job? Only Johnny Cash, of course.

BIG SCREEN, SMALL SCREEN, BOOKS AND NEWSPAPERS

# THE WRITTEN WORD

## Crossing Genres

Any list of films, television programs and books could easily contain 100 or more outstanding productions. The most difficult category even to broach is hardcover and softcover fiction. You can find the Civil War in every bookstore aisle, from history to biography to fiction. When authors are not writing historical nonfiction, they are placing their characters in the Civil War in love stories, thrillers and even science fiction. Whatever genre is your favorite as a reader is the best place to begin to be both entertained and absorbed in stories about the Civil War.

If the book is good historical fiction, you need not wonder *if* it will be made into a film—it's just a question of *when*, as with *Andersonville, Gettysburg* (the movie version of *The Killer Angels*) and many more.

When you select a stack of books for personal reading, start with James McPherson. His 900-page epic *Battle Cry of Freedom: The Civil War Era* won the Pulitzer Prize and reminds us how great it is when a talented historian is also a talented storyteller. He brings the Civil War, as they say, into your living room.

Whether you are a collector or "just a reader," try used and antiquarian bookstores, as well as the library, that incredibly ingenious idea of Ben Franklin's that allows you to read forever and not have to pay for the privilege!

## All the News...

While stocking your education/entertainment library with the Civil War, remember that there are also more sources than books and films. What better way to study every aspect of the war than with current magazines and journals dedicated to it? Scan the newsstands as well as the bookshelves.

Better yet, read what was said about the Civil War while it was happening—in Congress, in newspapers, in battle, in homes and cities, large and small. Newspapers of the time published from Atlanta to Richmond, Philadelphia to New York, and in dozens of cities in between tell the stories at every level of excitement and importance and tedium that made up the daily news during the Civil War.

The story of the *Monitor* and the *Merrimac*, of the surrender at Appomattox and the assassination of Abraham Lincoln could all be found in the *New York Times* nearly as quickly as newspapers bring us headlines today.

It may be quite tedious and time consuming to study American history as it was being written and occurring, but there is no better way for a reader or student of the Civil War to absorb the news than the way soldiers, farmers and plantation owners did in the 1860s. Immersing oneself chronologically in the news and commentary as it occurred is a rare opportunity to travel in your own quasi time machine.

## Camp and Outpost Duty for Infantry

The rear guard of any army advancing on the enemy need not be stronger than one twentieth part of the entire force. On a retreat, it should be not less than one eighth of the infantry, and as large a proportion of artillery and cavalry as can be used to advantage.

# A CIVIL WAR TIMELINE

A church service in a Union camp

cv/o

**May 24, 1856:** The unrest in Kansas escalates, and John Brown's followers drag five pro-slavery men from their homes and slash and cut them to death with swords.

**August 30, 1856:** Brown's 38 men battle more than 300 pro-slavery men, killing 20 and wounding 40. The furious anti-abolitionists attack and destroy the town of Pottawatomie, Kansas, but Brown, as the underdog, is immortalized throughout the North. These battles in Kansas represent another step toward inevitable civil war.

**October 16, 1859:** Brown expects thousands of slaves to join him, but has just five black men total—

only one an escaped slave—in an attack on the U.S. ammunition stores at Harpers Ferry, Virginia. The action results in Brown's trial and hanging, which helps to polarize the country even more.

**November 6, 1860:** Abraham Lincoln is elected as our country's 16th president, and the South has sworn that if he is elected, there will be secession and a civil war.

**December 20, 1860:** South Carolina fulfills the promise, becoming the first state to secede from the Union.

**January–February 1861:** Mississippi, Florida, Alabama, Georgia, Louisiana and Texas all secede.

**February 9, 1861:** Jefferson Davis is selected as the provisional president of the new Confederate States of America.

**March 4, 1861:** Lincoln is inaugurated as president, and he is faced with the insurmountable task of trying to hold the country together even as the Southern states have already begun establishing their own government and creating their own infrastructure.

**April 12, 1861:** Confederate troops fire on the island fortress of Fort Sumter, South Carolina, and it is hardly a battle; the Union troops there were refused supplies as they were isolated by the South and must surrender under the barrage of fire.

**July 21, 1861:** The North learns a huge lesson. The first real battle of the war takes place at Bull Run, or Manassas, Virginia, just 10 miles from Washington, DC. (Throughout the war, the North and South use different names much of the time to identify the battles.) Hundreds of the social elite of Washington ride out in carriages to picnic nearby and watch the conflict. They have no idea what is in store; the feeling is the Union troops will simply destroy the South. Instead, the carnage that was the Civil War begins, Southern troops overrun the North, and as the Northern forces retreat embarrassingly, all the picnicking citizenry is caught in the firing and flee. There's no indication, however, that any civilians were killed.

**August 6, 1861:** The U.S. Congress passes a Confiscation Act allowing Union troops to confiscate enemy property, including slaves.

**November 2, 1861:** George McClellan becomes general-in-chief of the Union army, replacing the aging Winfield Scott. There would be a great many firings and replacements of military leaders by Lincoln over the next four years. He was not the type of president to interfere, or to sit back and do nothing. He read incessantly to learn about military history and tactics and annoyed more than a few generals when he would not just accept their word on what should be done.

**January 15, 1862:** Lincoln names Edwin Stanton as his Secretary of War.

**February 6, 1862:** Ulysses S. Grant and fellow general Andrew Foote capture forts Henry and Donelson, which is significant in that it leads to the capture of Nashville. Union troops continually look for opportunities not only to defeat Southern troops, but also to capture strategic cities, especially strategic port cities, a goal from early in the war.

**March 9, 1862:** The world's first naval battle between ironclad ships takes place at Hampton Roads, Virginia, where the smaller, faster Union *Monitor* takes on the rebuilt *Merrimac*, which is now the CSS *Virginia*.

**April 6–7, 1862:** A huge battle—and bloodbath—takes place at Shiloh, Tennessee, where Confederate General Thomas "Stonewall" Jackson is given his nickname for his refusal to give ground.

**April 29, 1862:** Admiral Farragut and his fleet show that the navy can contribute mightily to the war effort, essentially making it possible for ground forces to move in and capture New Orleans.

**May 31, 1862:** The Battle of Seven Pines, Virginia, and Robert E. Lee, already the leading general from the war's outset is promoted to commander of the Army of Northern Virginia. This is the army that was formerly known by the same name as the Union's Army of the Potomac; it was changed so that each side would be called by a different name.

**July 22, 1862:** Lincoln, who had drafted the Emancipation Proclamation some time earlier, shows it to his cabinet for the first time.

**August 29, 1862:** The Second Battle of Manassas/Bull Run takes place.

**September 17, 1862:** McClellan defeats Lee at Antietam, Maryland, pushing Lee back toward the south.

**November 7, 1862:** Lincoln appoints Ambrose Burnside to replace McClellan as commander of the Army of the Potomac and finds that he's gone from a situation that he didn't like to one of having an apparently inept general in Burnside.

**December 13, 1862:** Union forces lose 2½ times the troops that the Confederates do at the Battle of Fredericksburg, Virginia.

**January 1, 1863:** Lincoln issues the Emancipation Proclamation.

**January 23, 1863:** Continuing the "revolving door" policy of commanders, Joseph Hooker replaces Burnside as commander of the Army of the Potomac.

**May 1–4, 1863:** The Battle of Chancellorsville, Virginia, hits the Confederates hardest as Stonewall Jackson is shot three times by his own troops, resulting in the immediate amputation of his arm. He dies shortly afterward of the effects of the wound combined with pneumonia, and Lee's best general—and perhaps the best general on either side—is lost.

**July 1–3, 1863:** The Battle of Gettysburg, Pennsylvania, becomes the pivotal battle of the war. As the Union prevails, Lee loses scores of officers (including numerous generals), and he is stopped in his push into Union territory.

**July 18, 1863:** The black regiment, the 54th Massachusetts, demonstrates courage in battle at Fort Wagner, South Carolina; this was the first actual combat for black troops in the war.

**September 19, 1863:** The Battle of Chickamauga, Georgia, takes place.

**November 19, 1863:** The Union cemetery at Gettysburg is dedicated, and Lincoln delivers a few appropriate remarks (just 272 words in about three minutes), which become the most famous speech in American history.

**March 9, 1864:** Grant is given the rank of lieutenant general in charge of all U.S. troops.

**May 4, 1864:** The Union army begins marching south with the goal of capturing Richmond, Virginia, the Southern capital.

**May 5–6, 1864:** One of the ugliest battles of the war takes place at The Wilderness in Virginia, an entangled forest of scrub growth and underbrush that makes movements and marching virtually impossible.

**June 1–3, 1864:** The Battle of Cold Harbor and the beginning of the long siege of Petersburg, Virginia, by Union troops takes place.

**September 2, 1864:** Sherman takes Atlanta after having burned his way to the city, following Grant's orders to destroy whatever is of value to the enemy, from crops and livestock to buildings and stores of goods.

**September 7, 1864:** Sherman tells the citizens of Atlanta to evacuate, and he subsequently burns the city.

**November 8, 1864:** Lincoln is reelected, certainly in part by switching his running mate from Hannibal Hamlin to the Southern Democrat, Andrew Johnson, in a move that ensures the country will have one of its worst presidents ever and reminding us that the vice president is, indeed, just a bullet away from being president.

**January 31, 1865:** The 13th Amendment to the Constitution of the United States is passed by the U.S. House of Representatives, banning slavery forevermore within the country.

**February 17, 1865:** Charleston is evacuated, and Sherman takes Columbia, South Carolina. The war is over for all intents and purposes…except for more killing, which hardly abates in the last several weeks of the war.

**April 9, 1865:** General Lee surrenders at the Appomattox Court House. Amnesty is offered to all rebel troops, and they are allowed to keep their horses and rifles, but must turn in their side arms. They are told to go home and begin the long march to normalcy.

**April 14, 1865:** Just five days after Lee's surrender, John Wilkes Booth, a very famous actor from a very famous acting family and unfortunately also a Southern zealot, shoots Lincoln fatally at Ford's Theater in Washington. William Seward is nearly killed in a simultaneous attack. Johnson becomes president, and the U.S. flag is once again raised at Fort Sumter.

**April 26, 1865:** Booth is cornered by Union troops and shot to death.

**April 26–May 26, 1865:** Various scattered Confederate troops surrender, the last some six-plus weeks after Appomattox.

**July 7, 1865:** Mary Surratt, an accomplice of Booth's in the assassination of Lincoln, becomes the first woman executed in the U.S. along with other convicted Booth conspirators.

# ABOUT THE AUTHOR

## Norman Bolotin

Norman Bolotin has written eight books about the Civil War, Chicago's 1893 World's Columbian Exposition and the Klondike Gold Rush. As partners in The History Bank, he and his wife, Christine Laing, developed the award-winning *Young Readers' History of the Civil War* for Penguin/Scholastic. They currently are expanding their museum and publishing studies previously distributed and sponsored in part by the American Association of Museums, Association of American Publishers, Ingram Book Co. and the University of Chicago. Bolotin, an expert in world's fairs, has curated exhibits, written catalogs and conducted analyses of the World's Columbian and Seattle's Century 21 expositions. Bolotin and Laing live in Woodinville, Washington.